The Stor

Clarence Whaite, *The Rainbow*, courtesy Nottingham Castle Museum and Art Gallery

THE STORY SO FAR:

The Manchester Academy of Fine Arts from 1859 to 2003

SHEILA DEWSBURY

2003
Manchester Academy of Fine Arts

First published 2003 by Manchester Academy of Fine Arts
The Portico Library
57 Mosley Street
Manchester M2 3HY
www.mafa.org.uk

ISBN no 0-9546440-0-x

Designed and produced by Janet Allan
Printed and bound by Titus Wilson & Son
Kendal

Contents

LIST OF ILLUSTRATIONS – *page* 6

SOURCES – 8

ACKNOWLEDGEMENTS – 8

PREFACE – 9

1 THE BEGINNING – 11

2 THE 1860s AND 1870s – 14

3 THE 1880s AND 1890s – 18

4 1900 TO 1918 – 28

5 THE 1920s – 31

6 THE 1930s – 42

7 1939 TO 1945 – 46

8 1945 TO 1960 – 51

9 THE 1960s – 62

10 THE 1970s AND 1980s – 67

11 THE 1990s – 73

12 2000 TO 2003 – 83

Presidents of the Manchester Academy of Fine Arts – 86

Members of the Manchester Academy of Fine Arts – 88

Index – 92

List of Illustrations

Clarence Whaite, *The Rainbow* — *frontispiece*

James Astbury Hammersley, *Mountains and Clouds* — *page* 12

William Percy, founder member of the Manchester Academy — 13

Anderson Hague, leader of the Manchester School — 14

Town Hall, Manchester, designed by Manchester Academician, Alfred Waterhouse — 15

Frederick Shields — 16

Ford Madox Brown, *The Establishment of Flemish Weavers in Manchester* — 17

Annie Swynnerton, *Portrait of Isabel Dacre* — 18

Manchester City Art Gallery — 19

Academy conversazione, 1883 — 20

Anderson Hague, *Millpool* — 21

Clarence Whaite, *Llyn Dylun* — 22

Charles Potter, *A Winter's Tale* — 23

John Cassidy, *Ship Canal Digger* — 24

William Stott of Oldham, *Venus Born of the Sea Foam* — 26

Emma Magnus, *Francesca* — 28

Florence Monkhouse, *A Manchester Waterway* — 29

The Unveiling of the Statue of Edward VII in Whitworth Park — 30

Elias Bancroft, *The Roder Bogen, Rothenburg, Bavaria* — 31

Francis Dodd, *The Interrogation of a German Soldier* — 33

Charles Tunnicliffe, *Ringed Plovers* — 34

Annie Swynnerton, *Mother and Child* — 35

Isabel Dacre, *Italian Women in Church* — 37

Francis Dodd, *Portrait of Henry Lamb* — 38

Elizabeth Chapma*n*, *St Ann's Square, Manchester* — 39

Academy members working from the figure at the Acomb Street studio — 40

L.S. Lowry, *An Organ Grinder* — 43

James Chettle, *War Memorial* — 45

Ethel Gabain, *The Weaver* — 47

Alan Brough, *Rebirth* — 48

Thomas Dugdale, *Wartime Scene* — 49

Ethel Gabain, *Cathode Ray Tubes*   50

Theodore Major, *Wigan Street*   51

Ian Grant, *Portrait of Margo Ingham*   52

William Turner, *St Mary's, Stockport*   54

James Fitton, *Tavern Brawl*   55

Terry McGlynn   57

L.S. Lowry, *The Cripples*   58

Ted Roocroft and Ian Thompson   60

Roger Hampson, *Domino Players*   61

Ted Roocroft, *Heavy Sow*   62

Harry Rutherford, *Mill Girls, Ashton*   64

Roger Hampson, *Miners*   65

L.S. Lowry with Ellis Shaw   67

Dawn Rowland, *Femme de Rocher*   70

Norman Jaques, *Rotting Tree Stump*   71

Ian Grant with an early self portrait   72

Glenys Latham, *Curled*   73

John McCombs, *Road Leading into Delph Village, Winter*   74

Paul Critchley, *The Balcony*   75

Paul Ritchie, *Bass Rock*   75

Peter Oakley, *Tableau: Histories and Mysteries*   76

Don McKinlay, *Janina*   77

Sheila Dewsbury, *Above Greenfield, Saddleworth*   78

Irene Halliday, *Still Life, Midsummer's Night, Oban*   79

Thompson Dagnall, *A Kirkby Kiss*   80

Julia Midgley, *Operation*   81

Ian Thompson, *Crown of Thorns*   82

Norman Jaques, *River Medlock, Charles Street, Manchester*   83

Alastair C. Adams, *Amy and Lucy*   84

Sources

The Archives of the Manchester Academy of Fine Arts
Biographies of artists held at Manchester Art Gallery
Clements, Keith, *Henry Lamb and His Friends,* Redcliffe Press, Bristol 1985
Davies, Peter, *A Northern School*, Redcliffe Press, Bristol 1989
Hartwell, Clare, *Pevsner Architectural Guides. Manchester*, Penguin Books 2001
Kidd, Alan, *Manchester*, Edinburgh University Press 1993
Klingender, Francis D., *Art and the Industrial Revolution,* Paladin, London 1947
Lord, Peter, *Clarence Whaite and the Welsh Art World. The Betws-y-coed Artists' Colony 1844–1914*, National Library of Wales 1998
Macdonald, Stuart, *The Royal Manchester Institute*
Manchester Town Hall Guide, Willow Publishing, Altrincham, Cheshire
Smith, Emma, *The Life and Work of Harry Rutherford 1903-1985,* Tameside MBC 1998
Taylor, Rod and Brian Edmondson, Interview with Ted Roocroft in 1981.
Wilenski, R.H., *A Miniature History of European Art*, Oxford University Press 1930

Illustrations for which no source is given come from the archives of the Manchester Academy of Fine Arts.

Acknowledgements

I would like to thank Neil Barrow, Keith Hamlett, Jan Green, Norman Jaques, Colin Jellicoe, Glenys Latham, Philip Livesey, Joan Livesey, John McCombs, Cliff Moorhouse and Christopher Rigby, also Melva Croal, Curator of Art at Manchester Art Gallery, and Curatorial Assistant, Sarah Skinner.

Every effort has been made by the author and publishers of this book to verify sources and copyright.

Preface

In 1823 the Society of Associated Artists of Manchester set in motion the establishment of an institution for the promotion of fine arts. The group, which often met at the premises of Thomas Dodd, an engraver and picture dealer, at 20 King Street wanted to 'further the cultivation of fine art and benefit Manchester artists'. They also needed an exhibition space, preferably with lantern light, and launched an appeal to raise funds for their project.

Manchester was in the thick of the Industrial Revolution and the people approached were a volatile mix of capitalist factory owners and merchants, cultured professionals and radical members of the rising middle classes. The artists' ideas caught their imagination and money poured in. Everyone wanted a chance to become a proprietor of the proposed institution, except the nobility. Lord de Tabley was the only aristocrat to offer support with a donation of 50 guineas. Other requests for help were sharply rebuffed. The old ruling classes were nervous about the social developments; the spectre of the French Revolution still hung in the air, and only four years previously the savage reaction to radical free thinkers had led to the Peterloo Massacre.

The new industrialists were unstoppable. Their enthusiasm for the new institution resulted in their taking the management out of the hands of the artists. They bought property around Spring Gardens and Thomas Dodd's house in King Street, but a legal dispute led to the entrance to number 20 being bricked up, to the chagrin of the artists who met there. Later Dodd left Manchester 'turned out of house and home by the success of his own project'. By then the artists had resigned their governing powers to business men.

In 1824 with the help of the Home Secretary, Robert Peel, the institution received royal patronage from the King, George IV, a keen supporter of the arts. Now a larger building to accommodate space for annual art exhibitions and lecture theatres was needed and land was acquired in the middle of Manchester's fashionable area on Mosley Street. Sir Charles Barry, who later designed the Houses of Parliament, was the architect. The building, which is now the Manchester Art Gallery, was finished in 1829 at a cost of £30,000.

The Royal Manchester Institution went on to initiate public art education and an annual exhibition of contemporary art second only to the Royal Academy. It would be another thirty years before a new generation of Manchester artists established a formal society, ironically under the auspices of the RMI.

In 1838 the Manchester School of Design, the first form of public art education in the city, originated in the RMI building in response to cotton manufacturers objecting to paying large sums of money to the French for designs for new fabrics. Although the emphasis was on design and craft, life classes were held and among the students were founders of the Manchester Academy and future presidents Robert Crozier and Clarence Whaite. When life models were abolished for a period owing to the oversensitive attitude of some RMI governors – this was around the time Etty's painting *The Sirens and Ulysses* was hung face to the wall in the same building – the frustrated students started their own life classes in an attic in King Street. They called themselves the Roman Bricks.

The Association of Artists was still in existence, meeting informally to sketch and discuss art, and in 1849 it was given a room for study in the RMI building. Unfortunately it was close to the chemical laboratory in the basement and the air was 'tainted with noxious fumes'. It was probably the same laboratory that was still paying rent in 1888, when its proximity to the valuable paintings of the City Art Gallery was a cause for concern.

Meanwhile the fortunes of the School of Design foundered and it became bankrupt. Unable to pay the rent, it moved out of Mosley Street for a period, but in 1849 James Astbury Hammersley, the driving force behind the establishment of the Manchester Academy was made headmaster. It was a turning point. Within five years the school was renamed The Manchester School of Art, more fine art including life classes was introduced, and with seven hundred pupils on the roll Hammersley soon moved it back to Mosley Street.

By now there was a lively body of artists working around the King Street–St Ann's Square area of the city. There were engravers, lithographers, theatrical designers and landscape and portrait painters thriving on the knock-on effect of the boom in the cotton trade. Imports of raw cotton had risen to 872 million lbs a year by 1851, but not all shared the prosperity: the official life expectancy of labourers and mechanics was seventeen years.

Some future Academicians such as Frederick Shields, who later won national recognition, had difficulty finding work; he once walked to Liverpool and back in search of employment. Others, like William Percy who became a successful portrait painter, 'painted anything'. He records early morning visits to Shudehill Market carrying his paints, which he had ground and burnt himself, in bladders. 'Sometimes', he wrote, 'the bladder would burst and there would be an awful mess.'

CHAPTER 1

The Beginning

In 1857, the year after the Crimean War ended, Queen Victoria and Prince Albert came to Manchester to open the Art Treasures Exhibition at Old Trafford, and to unveil the statue of the Queen at Peel Park, Salford.

David Chadwick, the Salford Borough Treasurer, had the idea of staging an exhibition for the occasion of work by artists from the area, and James Hammersley organised the show. The Prince already knew Hammersley because he had commissioned him to paint his birthplace, the Castle of Rosenau, nine years previously. He bought five paintings at the Salford exhibition, and expressed interest when James Hammersley spoke to him about proposals to establish a Manchester Academy of Fine Arts.

Inspired by this encouragement and the success of the exhibition the Manchester Association of Artists held a meeting at the RMI in May the same year. It was felt that the profession was disunited and needed a common centre for classes, meetings and exhibitions. Out of forty-two men present a committee of ten was elected to work out a draft constitution, and to approach the Council of the RMI for accommodation in the Mosley Street building. They sought advice and received 'most cordial assistance' from established Academies in London and Edinburgh, and those in Europe including Paris, Lyons and Munich, using the information gathered as a basis for a constitution. On 12 March 1858 the *Manchester Guardian* reported 'A meeting of artists of this city was held last night in the lecture hall of the Royal Manchester Institution for the purpose of considering the establishing of a Manchester Academy of Fine Arts.'

It was proposed that the Academy would promote an annual exhibition and undertake the tuition of students. Members would be elected on presentation of a specimen of their work, and professional painters, sculptors and architects would be admitted. There would be Academicians, Associates and Students. Numbers would not be limited and either sex would be admitted, but it would be some years before women applied for membership.

On 1 June 1859 the governors of the RMI resolved that the Association of Artists in Manchester, from now on to be known as the Manchester Academy of Fine Arts, should have free access to the building and occupy rooms for study and meetings, and should pay £50 a year towards general expenses. This sum was to be waived in return for the Academy taking over the organisation of the annual autumn Exhibition of Works of Modern Art staged by the RMI since 1829. This was the most prestigious showcase for contemporary art outside London, and was

James Astbury Hammersley, *Mountains and Clouds*, the scene from the top of Loughrigg, Westmorland. Courtesy of Manchester Art Gallery

timed to coincide with the end of the Royal Academy show so that artists could send work directly north. Most of the painters and sculptors from Manchester had been exhibiting in the autumn show since its inauguration, and in 1859 Clarence Whaite was awarded the silver medal for his painting *Expulsion from Paradise*.

Later the same month James Hammersley and John Lamont Brodie had an interview with Prince Albert at Windsor Castle to inform him of developments, and at the same time 'presented a memorial through the Home Secretary to the Queen for the grant of certain privileges.'

The first ten Academicians, mostly men in their thirties and early forties, were elected by ballot. In order of voting they were:

William Percy, a portrait painter with bright eyes and a great jolly laugh;

James Hammersley, the first President, a landscape painter, and a genial man of large ideas;

John Bostock, a portrait painter;

Robert Crozier, a gentle man with a piping voice but robust frame, a painter of domestic subjects;

William Hull, a landscape painter with a natural sense of beauty;
Henry Calvert, the first Treasurer, a fashionable painter of animals
and sporting subjects;
Charles Mitchell, a watercolourist;
John Lamont Brodie, the first Secretary, a painter of historical genre
landscape and figure;
William Knight Keeling, a portrait and figure painter;
George Anthony, the first Literary Secretary, a landscape painter and
art critic.

On 14 November 1859 a certificate of registration was received and at
a meeting the following day Hammersley announced that all negotiations had been completed and the Manchester Academy of Fine Arts
was now a fact.

William Percy, founder member of the Manchester Academy

Sadly, celebrations were marred by the sudden death of George
Anthony, who, writing under the name Gabriel Tinto, was the art crit-
ic of the *Manchester Guardian*. His place was taken by the man sharing the same number of
votes for tenth place, Clarence Whaite, who was to become one of the legendary figures of the
Academy. In the following months membership rose to around twenty-five, an average which
remained for approximately ten years, with a dozen or so associates and a growing number of
students.

The Academy organised three Autumn Exhibitions with great success, hanging over eight
hundred works and doubling sales. Then there was an abrupt end. It was not to be responsible
for any further RMI exhibitions. The reason for this is not clear, but the timing coincided with
official disapproval by the RMI Governors of James Hammersley who was establishing a lucra-
tive practice as a professional painter which it was felt clashed with his duties as headmaster. In
1862 he resigned as head of the Art School and President of the Academy, becoming an honorary member before leaving for Bristol. Two wider catastrophes had occurred: the death of
Prince Albert in 1861, followed by the Queen withdrawing from public life, thus robbing the
Academy of any kudos royal patronage would bring, and the American Civil War. Imports of raw
cotton, the life blood of rich and poor, ceased.

The Academy remained on good terms with the RMI. Members continued to exhibit at the
Autumn Show, sometimes forming part of selection or hanging committees. They were given
free use of rooms for classes, meetings and space for future exhibitions. The first one in 1865
was a small semi-private affair with barely a page of press coverage, but over the next ten years
there would be an extraordinary growth in the significance of the Academy's exhibitions.

CHAPTER 2

The 1860s and 1870s

The next exhibition was held in 1869, this time in Spring to allow artists to send work on to the Royal Academy; the Annual Exhibition has been held around this time of year ever since. It was customary to work from the figure during the winter and to paint landscape directly from nature in the summer, the further away from the filth and darkness of industrial Lancashire the better. The Yorkshire Dales and the Lake District were inspirational – William Hull was living at Dove Cottage only five years after Wordsworth had died – and several members were already visiting North Wales, where an artists' colony led by David Cox flourished at Betws-y-coed in the Conwy Valley.

A twenty-three-year-old Clarence Whaite had first painted in Llanberis in 1851. The spell Snowdonia cast on him when he wrote '... how its grandeur overpowers me – if I could paint the extent of my feelings...' stayed with him undiminished over the next sixty years. He painted high in the mountains sometimes staying all winter in a wooden hut cum mobile studio erected near Capel Curig. His painting *The Rainbow* won the Gold Medal at the RMI Exhibition in 1862, and is now in the collection of Nottingham Art Gallery.

As early as 1863 the *Manchester Guardian* had reported '... an uprising of a Manchester School...' which blossomed in the late 60s and 70s when a group of enthusiastic young men led by Anderson Hague was influenced by fellow Academician Joseph Knight. Hague with others including Richard Gay Somerset, George Hayes, Charles Meredith and later Frederick Jackson

Anderson Hague, leader of the Manchester School

and Rose Magnus, were inspired by the Barbican painters, especially Corot. Their atmospheric landscapes caused the periodical, *The Critic*, to declare, 'A school of artists has appeared comet like before the Manchester public.' But their use of soft grey/greens and subdued tones brought adverse reaction from some people, and it was alleged that they could not draw because there were no sharp outlines or detail in their work. Their frequent use of palette knife was 'anathema'. Webster, writing in the *Manchester Examiner*, used the name Manchester School jokingly, and it was repeated in derision by hostile critics, but the title was adopted by the artists and used to their advantage. Founder member William Percy simply said of Anderson Hague 'He paints as a bird sings'.

Luckily landscape was popular with potential buyers.

Contemporary Manchester subjects did not appeal, not solely because Ruskin said that no good painting could ever come out of Manchester as the sun was obscured by dirt and smoke, but because people wanted some escape from the harshness of their surroundings.

Throughout the 1860s and 70s the Academy grew and prospered. The Annual Exhibition held in the two large galleries and the smaller South gallery received increasing press coverage, and the opening soirées or conversaziones became one of the highlights of the Manchester social scene attracting up to nine hundred people at a time. The artists, it was said years later, could be recognised by their unconventional dress with 'the strangest coats, the queerest hats and the longest hair'.

The general public was not admitted until 1874 when the first catalogue was produced. Neither the Academy nor the RMI exhibitions were free, although the RMI experimented with its big autumn exhibition by opening free on Sundays in 1879. Over eleven Sundays 51,682 of the 'very poor' visited the gallery.

All the members were professional; the fact that many supplemented their income by various forms of teaching did not compromise this status. The question of admitting amateurs had been raised in 1865 and again in 1882, but it was felt that the 'lay elements' would spoil the market. In 1913 the proposal was 'vehemently opposed' at a stormy meeting, but only four years later in 1917, in a rapidly changing society, it was decided that amateurs could apply for membership.

Most of the members were painters; there is no evidence of sculptors although this would soon change dramatically. Some distinguished architects were Academicians, and many buildings in and around Manchester are the work of these men. Perhaps the most well-known is Alfred Waterhouse who submitted the winning design for the new Town Hall in 1868. The following year the foundation stone was laid at the base of the clock tower, the pinnacle stone of the spire was laid in 1875 and the gilt ball on top of that a month later. The Town Hall is now a Grade One Listed Building.

Waterhouse also designed Strangeways Prison and the University buildings on Oxford Road. From 1876 to 1878 he was responsible for restoration and alterations at Chetham's School, and between 1887 and 1889 he restored and remodelled St Ann's Church in St Ann's Square.

One of the earliest Academicians, Edward Salomons, designed the Sephardic Synagogue in Cheetham Hill in 1874. It is now also the Manchester Jewish Museum and a Grade Two Listed Building.

Town Hall, Manchester, designed by Manchester Academician, Alfred Waterhouse

Frederick Shields

Alfred Darbyshire, a Council member and Trustee of the Academy, designed the Palace Theatre in 1891. The building was altered in 1913 and beige tiles were added in 1956, but the splendid interior remains. Darbyshire had considerable experience in designing fireproof cotton mills, and, with Henry Irving, pioneered fireproof safety theatre designs. He worked extensively in the theatre in costume and set design and even 'trod the boards' himself, playing Polonius to Irving's *Hamlet*.

Frederick Shields worked with Waterhouse on the restoration of St Ann's Church, drawing up a complete scheme for the whole church based on the theme of The Shepherd. The three stained glass windows above the altar are his design. Earlier in 1877 it was he who suggested that his friend, Ford Madox Brown, should share with him the execution of twelve murals depicting the history of Manchester in the new Town Hall. Shields later withdrew because he moved to London. Madox Brown took on the whole project, moved to Manchester and began a long association with the city during the fifteen years it took to complete the work. He used friends and their families as models for many of the figures; Shields is said to be the model for Wycliffe. The murals reflect Victorian values, emphasising the importance of Christianity, non-conformism, science, invention, education, trade and the textile industry – a proposal to include the Peterloo Massacre was too sensitive to contemplate. Madox Brown made many friends at the Academy and was elected Honorary Member in 1882.

Education was central to the activities of the Academy; students worked alongside members and associates in the life rooms at the RMI in Mosley Street, and in 1867 the President, William Keeling, reported that instead of having to hire costumes from London for the draped figure classes, there was enough money to have their own costumes made. He regretted that access to professional nude models was difficult in provincial towns, but with more funds it would now be easier to hire those available.

The attitude to the nude as a subject for a finished work was ambivalent; the naked nymphs and various immortals found on large canvases were considered respectable as long as they were detached from real life. In 1870 a journalist referring to a painting with a nude figure by a 'foreign artist' in the RMI exhibition wrote 'Godesses may be forgiven the absence of garments, but an undressed modern Delilah stretched on a hearthrug can serve no useful purpose. It is photographic and nastily so.'

It was not unusual for women to receive art education and to exhibit work, but it was socially taboo for both sexes to work from life at the same time. No wonder newspaper articles expressed

Ford Madox Brown, *The Establishment of Flemish Weavers in Manchester AD 1363, visit of Philippa of Hainault, Queen of Edward III to them* (reduced version for the Town Hall murals. Courtesy of Manchester Art Gallery)

'shock and disbelief' when in 1874 women applied to become members of the Academy. An unnamed journalist wrote 'Ladies would not care to avail themselves of full rights of membership' as it would mean studying from the nude in mixed classes, and it would be 'particularly indelicate as the nudes would be alive, unlike the dead ones that the ladies of the medical school in Edinburgh had recently been granted permission to work with'.

Although the question about the suitability of women attending the draped figure class had been discussed at an Academy meeting in 1869, it had not been pursued. There was no exclusion of women in the original constitution, but the rules stipulated attendance at classes before work could be exhibited. The difficulties were overcome by the addition of a class for ladies only, and in 1875 nine women were elected members: Annie Robinson (later Swynnerton), Emily Robinson, Julia Robinson, Emily Gertrude Thompson, Mary Southworth, Ann Crozier, Eleanor Wood, Annie Hasling and Isabel Dacre. Known as 'lady exhibitors', several had studied in Manchester before going on to the Slade, then to ateliers in Paris. It was recorded at the AGM that the combined influence of both sexes would strengthen the Academy.

In 1880 an article in the *Manchester Guardian* called for the Academy to abolish the 'invidious distinction' of referring to women as 'lady exhibitors' and consider them members or associates. Four years later this proposal was adopted unanimously at the AGM, and women were elected on the same terms as men – although they were not eligible for office. This changed over the next few years; women became council members and regularly served on the hanging committee.

Annie Swynnerton, *Portrait of Isabel Dacre*. Courtesy of Manchester Art Gallery

CHAPTER 3
The 1880s and 1890s

It was becoming an embarrassment that unlike other prominent cities Manchester had no free public art gallery. Several bequests to the city had already gone to galleries in other towns because there were no facilities for keeping, let alone exhibiting, works of art. In 1876 the RMI offered its building and art collection to the Corporation, but it was thought unsuitable, possibly because warehouses had replaced the affluent residential and leisure district around Mosley Street, Princess Street and Portland Street.

Several options were considered: if the RMI merged with the Botanical Society and moved to Old Trafford the Mosley Street building could be sold by the Corporation and a new gallery built.

Manchester City Art Gallery

The School of Art was planning to move from the building to new premises, and it was suggested that an art gallery could adjoin it on proposed land next to Chorlton Town Hall. In 1877 the School, assisted by public donation, and continuing to operate under the auspices of the RMI, bought land at Cavendish Street, and there was some discussion about a gallery being built near it in the All Saints area.

By 1880 the dilemma was near to resolution. At a council meeting of the RMI it was proposed 'To transfer the entire property as a public gift to the City of Manchester'. In 1882 the RMI made a gift of its building to the Corporation 'for the establishment of a Public Art Gallery'. The paintings and sculptures donated at the same time formed the nucleus of a growing permanent collection on display free to the public; the selling exhibitions of the Academy and the RMI still charged an admission fee.

Robert Crozier, President of the Academy during this period of transition, later said, 'While negotiations for the transfer were pending, the Academy was anxious… the future of Manchester Academy was in no way clear…', but after a meeting with the Mayor at which a 'pleasant atmosphere' was noted it was agreed that the Annual Exhibition should continue.

Alterations were to take place in the rooms used for life classes. The Academy was offered accommodation in the basement, but chose to re-locate the students to premises on Brazenose Street.

The first event held in the City Art Gallery was the Annual Academy Exhibition in Spring 1883. The *Manchester Evening News* reported that it was a strong show with genuine honest work. During the run of the exhibition 'Everyone who was anyone' came to a lecture on Art, Wealth and Riches given by William Morris to the Academy and Manchester Literary Society.

In the 1880s the Manchester School flourished with the use of brighter colour and an expressive response to nature. Ironically its 'undisputed leader', Anderson Hague, and several Academicians including Charles Potter, William Meredith, Henry Measham, George Hayes, William Artingstall, Richard Gay Somerset

Academy conversazione, 1883

Anderson Hague, *Millpool*. Courtesy of Manchester Art Gallery

Clarence Whaite, *Llyn Dylun*. Courtesy of Manchester Art Gallery

and Clarence Whaite were by then living more or less permanently in the Conwy area of North Wales, where they painted in the open countryside, often incorporating figures in the landscape. The paintings they sent back to Manchester for the annual exhibitions form an important contribution to Victorian painting.

Anderson Hague worked mostly around the Deganwy area whilst Clarence Whaite preferred the mountainous region of Snowdonia. Charles Potter from Oldham lived at Tal-y-Bont. His painting *A Winter's Tale* was bought from the Academy exhibition of 1881 for £150 by James Tweedale, who gave it to Oldham Free Library. It was hoped that this first work of art secured by the town would prove the beginning of a local art collection.

On 12 November 1881 these men attended a meeting at the Llandudno Junction Hotel to discuss the creation of a Welsh Academy. The Manchester Academicians were able to give expert

Charles Potter, *A Winter's Tale*. Courtesy of Gallery Oldham

advice on the running of such an organisation and eight of them became founder members of the Cambrian Academy which was granted royal patronage the following year with the help of Gladstone, the Prime Minister, who had a love of Welsh landscape painting.

Since then over thirty Manchester Academicians have been members of the Royal Cambrian Academy based in Conwy. Clarence Whaite was President from 1885 to 1912, and Owen Bowen was President from 1947 to 1953. Iola Spafford, the only contemporary artist to belong to both Academies, is among several MAFA members who continue to work in North Wales, sometimes exhibiting in the Royal Cambrian Summer Exhibition.

To celebrate Queen Victoria's Jubilee in 1887 the Royal Jubilee Exhibition was held in a pur-pose-built domed pavilion at Old Trafford. Coincidentally future Academician L.S. Lowry was born in the area on 1 November the same year. During the six months it was open there were 4,153,724 visitors. Fifty years of British Art were celebrated in fourteen galleries. Thomas Agnew of the Manchester-based art dealers and chairman of the organising committee asked members of the Academy to exhibit one work each, but the paintings were scattered and 'skyed'

John Cassidy,
Ship Canal Digger.
Courtesy of
Manchester Art
Gallery

... 'almost out of eye shot' according to the many letters of recrimination in the press.

Not all Academy involvement was acrimonious: Clarence Whaite's painting of Thirlmere won great acclaim. Mancunians were specially interested as the landscape depicted was about to be changed to provide the city with water to continue the fight against cholera and typhoid endemic among the poor; Ford Madox Brown, who painted gigantic figures to decorate the inside of the dome, wrote 'I had the assistance of four young ladies, extremely vigorous figure painters from the Manchester Academy of Fine Arts who had studied in Paris... [they] worked with skill and energy... from the top of a ladder to sitting on the floor.' And in one room a young sculptor, John Cassidy, was at work making up to two hundred heads in clay from life using the visitors as models.

Cassidy was the son of a farmer from Slane in County Meath. His outstanding artistic talent had led him to Manchester to study ten years previously at the age of seventeen. He was elected to full membership of the Academy in 1888 and the following year his bronze figure *Ship Canal Digger* was bought by the City Art Gallery. Although the sculptor, Warrington Wood, was an honorary member, it is probable that John Cassidy was the first sculptor to become an ordinary member of the Academy. Any lack of involvement in this area of art was ended. Many examples of his work including the sculptures of John and Henriquetta Rylands in the Rylands Library, the statue of Ben Brierely at Queen's Park and King Edward VII in Whitworth Park are public legacies. His figure group, *Adrift*, sited for many years in Piccadilly Gardens was Manchester's first modern non-portrait outdoor sculpture.

The vibrant art scene in Europe enticed several members of the Academy. After studying in Munich Arthur Wasse settled in Rothenburg, Bavaria. Elias and Louisa Bancroft were frequent visitors to the same village. The arrival of Impressionism then Post Impressionism caused artists to migrate to Paris; some like William Stott of Oldham, 'a wayward man of genius' lived there for a period. He had adopted the name of his home town to avoid confusion with a fellow Academician, Edward Stott RA from Rochdale. William Stott was said to be a strikingly original character, and his work was sometimes ridiculed by contemporary critics – his portrayal of Venus in one painting was described as 'More like a fairy with less clothes on than usual'. Although he won recognition in Europe, his reputation in England was not fully realised until several years after his early death at sea.

Many Academicians studied at ateliers; one of the most popular was M. Julien's where professors including Bouguereau and Lefebre taught. Models worked from 8 am to 12 noon and 1 pm to 5 pm, keeping the same pose for one week. A letter from a 'Manchester Man' to the press about his experience as a student there described a cacophony of noise from around a hundred people of all nationalities working in one room shouting, singing and telling dirty jokes in different languages. The air was

William Stott of Oldham, *Venus Born of the Sea Foam*, 'an ambitious fusion
of myth and plein air realism'. Courtesy of Gallery Oldham. Whistler's mistress, the painter,
Maud Franklin, was the model for Venus

thick with the smell of sweat and smoke from strong French tobacco, and the walls were covered with splashes of paint and rude caricatures.

In 1891 there was a 'serious crisis in management' at the Academy when the discovery of irregularities in funds caused by the lack of book-keeping resulted in the resignation of the Treasurer. He was forced to 'realise on his own house and private effects' to reimburse the Academy. Trustees were appointed, and the Academy was registered as a specially authorised society under the Friendly Societies Act of 1875. Financial arrangements were tightened; both Treasurer and Secretary would sign cheques from then on.

Members of the public were invited to become Annual Subscribers in 1892. For 1 guinea they were allowed free admission to all exhibitions and functions. People interested in art thus had the opportunity to be in closer contact with artists and their work and take an active part in the well-being of the Academy. The support of the Subscribers has played a vital role and continues to do so today.

Towards the end of the century there was a reshuffle in the officers of the Academy. Clarence Whaite was elected President in 1892. He was simultaneously President of the Royal Cambrian Academy until his death in 1912. Reg Barber, who won the Gold Medal at the Paris Salon in 1894, held the newly-created post of Vice-President for fourteen years. John Cassidy became Treasurer and managed the finances for the next twenty-six years. In 1894 Elias Bancroft took on the job of Secretary, a post he held for twenty-nine years until his retirement when it was taken over by his wife, Louisa, who held it for a further sixteen years. Emma Magnus became Literary Secretary in 1895 and was responsible for the Academy archives for the next thirty-seven years until 1932.

No one realised then that the stability created in the management of the Academy by the appointment of most of these people was crucial in carrying it through one of the most turbulent periods in modern history.

In the early 90s the running of the Autumn Exhibition was taken over by the City Art Gallery Committee. The format of the exhibition was changing with new social developments, and the RMI was changing too: its great pioneering work of public education passed to the responsibility of the City Council, and although it continued with lectures and donations of prizes and free scholarships to MAFA students its importance was diminishing.

The management of the Manchester School of Art had been transferred to the Corporation in 1892. Developments in public art education led to the gradual shift of students relying on Academy classes; in 1897 out of 5,000 art students nationwide 2,030 of them were in Manchester.

The policy of admitting students from the Art School, Chetham's School and Salford Technical School to Academy exhibitions at reduced rates was gratefully acknowledged in letters to the council from the heads of these establishments.

Emma Magnus, *Francesca*

Florence
Monkhouse,
*A Manchester
Waterway*

CHAPTER 4

1900 to 1918

The Annual Spring Exhibition flourished. It was open for up to eight weeks and in 1907 there were over 1,000 at the Private View. Evening soirées or conversaziones were literally glittering occasions, when ladies wore chiffon, lace, taffeta and brocade; the Mayoress of Salford appeared in a Parisian gown with a diamond tiara and necklace. Military bands played and the Cathedral Choir sang. In 1909 for the fiftieth anniversary of the foundation of the Academy there was a Jubilee Dinner at the Town Hall, and a special exhibition at the City Art Gallery of work by past and present members.

MANCHESTER'S STATUE OF KING EDWARD.

The Unveiling of the Statue of Edward VII in Whitworth Park.
Daily Mail photograph

The President, Clarence Whaite, one of the great Victorian painters, died in 1912. The *Manchester Guardian* paid tribute to his 'simplicity of nature, geniality and cheerfulness'. Eleven years previously the Art Gallery had celebrated his seventieth birthday with an exhibition of over a hundred paintings from its own permanent collection and those in other galleries including Liverpool, Leeds and Nottingham.

John Ely succeeded him. He is the only architect to have been President. His best-known work is the design of St Mary's Hospital on Oxford Road, but he was also responsible for work on offices at Dean Clough, Halifax which has links with some present Academicians who use studio space or exhibition facilities there.

Manchester subjects were increasingly popular. The canal wharf at Castlefield was described as 'a veritable artists' mecca'. Sometimes the number of easels obstructed the tow ropes slung between the horses and barges, but the occasional entanglements were taken by everyone, including the bargees, in good humour.

Academicians travelled increasingly to France, Germany, Italy and Greece. In the winter of 1913 Frederick Jackson worked in Russia, producing thirty landscapes, all completed in the open air 'under trying conditions of temperature'. The critics thought the paintings offered a new knowledge of the charm of Russia under snow. This impossibly romantic view together with everything else would soon be shattered.

The Edwardian era had ended in 1910 with the death of Edward VII and the accession of his son, George V. In October 1913 a statue of King Edward by John Cassidy was unveiled outside the Whitworth Gallery. In a speech at the unveiling the late King was admired as he had fostered friendly relations with France and had 'bettered the understanding that existed with the German Empire'.

Ten months later at the outbreak of the First World War Elias and Louisa Bancroft were trapped in Germany. They were painting as usual in Rothenburg and had not bothered to take passports. The Burgermeister gave them papers of safe passage stating that they were artists not spies, and they began a hair-raising journey home amid a mêlée of troops, field guns, Italian refugees and ordinary, slightly bewildered, Germans returning from their holidays. These people proved friendly and helpful when jittery officials wanted to arrest the Bancrofts who eventually arrived several days later at Folkstone in a state of exhaustion.

In Manchester the war effort was under way: Academician Eleanor Wood instigated a War Fund Art Union Lottery sanctioned by the Board of Trade at the City Art Gallery. The sale of 48,000 tickets raised £1,760.

Many Academicians were now involved in the war. Some of the older ones were in the Territorial Army, whilst the younger ones became soldiers or nurses, but the next Annual

Elias Bancroft, *The Roder Bogen, Rothenburg, Bavaria*

Exhibition was held as usual in Spring 1915.

By the following year the realisation of the devastating effects of this war was recorded in the *Manchester Guardian*: 'The old world came to an end sometime in 1914 and the new world has done nothing yet for art except shatter it.'

In a lecture at the University Lawrence Haward, Curator of the City Art Gallery, said that war periods of the past had produced great paintings and literature, but this war was different, it was no longer a romantic adventure. He hoped that genuine art might result 'when all the welter of the present war, all the bitterness and the courage, the folly and the waste have been gathered into perspective...'.

In 1916 John Ely died, and Tom Mostyn, a 'dominating energetic person' was elected President. He introduced a spirit of reform, and the proposal to accept amateurs as members was unanimously adopted in 1917. The old criterion of electing professionals only was waived in recognition of the fine quality of work produced by artists from all walks of life, and the changes brought additional benefits to the Academy.

By 1917 the logistics of staging the Annual Exhibition were formidable. The railways, the most convenient mode of transport for artists, could no longer carry paintings or sculpture. Not much new work was being produced, but that previously exhibited by past and present members was mustered by the Secretary, Elias Bancroft, and during weeks of 'intense cold and dark' the exhibition was held as usual. The *Manchester City News* reported 'the difficulties of getting together even the nucleus of an exhibition were overwhelming', but 'it would have been a calamity if the continuity of these Spring Exhibitions had been broken'.

Some Academicians became official war artists. Francis Dodd made portraits of leaders including General Smuts and Admiral Jellicoe which were reproduced in newspapers and used as a valuable part of British propaganda in the USA. He worked on the Western Front, record-ing powerful images such as the interrogation of a German soldier by British officers, sketched on a crumpled scrap of paper and now in the collection of the Imperial War Museum. He was commissioned to record life on minesweepers and submarines, an experience which gave him a lasting respect for the men who served in them.

Thomas Dugdale from Blackburn had joined the Yeomanry in 1910 because he was a good rider. His regiment was mobilised on 4 August 1914, and soon he found himself at Gallipoli. Although he was not an official war artist, Generals Allenby and Barrow relieved him of duties in order to make visual records in the Sinai Desert, the Balkans, Palestine and Syria. Many of these sketches are in the Imperial War Museum.

At the end of the Great War Sheridan Knowles was commissioned by the French Government to paint the Peace Conference at Versailles. A future honorary member, Sir William Orpen, painted the signing of the Peace Treaty.

In 1918 reform continued at the Academy with the introduction of free entry to the Annual Exhibitions after the first week. This was a radical change to what had been an exclusive event, thus opening up access to everyone regardless of class or income. The subsequent soaring rise in visitors to the exhibition from just over 2,000 to 23,000 by 1920 could not wholly be attributed to post-war jubilation.

Francis Dodd, *The Interrogation of a German Soldier*. Courtesy of the Imperial War Museum

Charles Tunnicliffe, *Ringed Plovers*. © Estate of C.F. Tunnicliffe

CHAPTER 5

The 1920s

There was a period of transition after the war with some friction between the traditional-
ists and those with a more modern approach, but the *Manchester Guardian* noted
'renewed energies' with the two approaches gaining from one another. Anderson Hague,
a member for over forty years and Vice-President of the Royal Cambrian Academy, had died in
1916. The City Art Gallery staged a Memorial Exhibition of his work in 1919, the same year
one of the Academy students, L. S. Lowry, exhibited three pieces, including a pencil drawing for

Annie Swynnerton,
Mother and Child.
Painted in 1886 when she
was living in Rome. Courtesy of
Manchester Art Gallery

4 guineas. Young members like Bertram Nicholls, fresh from his exploits in the Kite and Balloon section of the RAF, returned full of vigour. Charles Cundall, who had just taught himself to paint with his left hand after being wounded in his right, was elected to full membership in 1923, and Charles Tunnicliffe, painting from a woodshed lit by an oil lamp in Macclesfield, joined in 1929. Both men later became Royal Academicians.

Under Francis Dodd's Presidency in the early twenties the rules were changed to allow the election of eminent artists without their having to submit work. Sir William Orpen, Henry Lamb, Sydney Lee, Charles Holmes and Terrick Williams were among the new Honorary Members. By 1925 the *Daily Mail* reported that the Academy was 'progressive and growing in strength'.

Manchester was the cradle of the Suffragette movement, and following the General Election of 1918 when women over thirty were allowed to vote, their gradual emancipation was reflected at the Academy. Original women members back in 1874 had been barred from office; by 1923 the posts of Treasurer, Secretary and Literary Secretary were all held by women, but it would be almost seventy years before a woman was elected President.

One of these original members, Annie Swynnerton, was elected an Associate of the Royal Academy in 1922 at the age of seventy-six. She was the first woman to receive Academic honours since 1768 when Angelica Kaufmann and Mary Moser became foundation members of the RA. The City Art Gallery held an exhibition of her work to celebrate, and hosted a Civic Reception.

Annie, born Annie Robinson in Hulme, had studied at the Manchester School of Art in the 1870s and later with Isabel Dacre in Paris and Rome, where she met and married the sculptor, Joseph Swynnerton. They lived there for many years until his death when she returned to England to work from her studio in London. She was encouraged by Singer Sergeant and Rodin who both bought work. She loved painting children in natural settings, and, like Turner, adored the sun; her work was often symbolic and allegorical with vibrating effects of light achieved by free use of broken colour. Her formal portraits, notably one of Henry James, caught the character of the sitter, and the one of the Revd William Gaskell, commissioned by the Portico Library, is in Manchester Art Gallery's collection. She painted successfully to the end of her life at the age of eighty-eight, when because of failing eyesight the pictures were a shimmering veil of colour with sweeping, sharply drawn outlines.

In 1925 Margaret Pilkington, an Associate of the Academy who had studied like her contemporary, Lowry, under Valette at the Manchester School of Art and in Academy life classes exhibited a wood engraving for 1 guinea. An accomplished painter and printmaker, she used her wealth and position to benefit the cultural life of the region. The same year she was invited to join the Whitworth Art Gallery Committee, becoming its representative on the City Art Gallery

Isabel Dacre, *Italian Women in Church*. Courtesy of Manchester Art Gallery

Francis Dodd, *Portrait of Henry Lamb*. Courtesy of Manchester Art Gallery

Committee, the first woman to serve on either one. She was elected to full membership in 1926. As a child her portrait had been painted by another Academy icon, Isabel Dacre.

Susan Isabel Dacre was honoured in 1927 at the age of eighty-four by a testimonial exhibition at the City Art Gallery. It was arranged by Past President, Francis Dodd, who had been a close friend since his early days in Manchester when he was invited to visit her for two weeks and stayed for fourteen years. He never forgot the encouragement she gave at the start of his career; long afterwards he said that any civilisation he had managed to acquire came from his friendship with 'that remarkable creature'.

Isabel was born in Leamington Spa in 1844, came to Manchester as an infant and was educated at a convent in Salford, but would never speak of her early life. As a thirteen-year-old at the time of the Art Treasures Exhibition in 1857 she lived at the Stamford Arms in Altrincham where her mother was landlady. One of the guests was Anthony Trollope who spent every morning 'writing, writing, surrounded by a litter of papers' before visiting the exhibition in the afternoons. He lent her the manuscript to read; it was the finishing chapters of *Barchester Towers*. The next year she went to Paris as a pupil, became a governess and fell in love with France and all things French, so much so that after being sent home with other foreigners at the outbreak of the Franco-Prussian War in 1870 she returned too soon and was forced to fight at the barricades before being 'extricated from a perilous situation'.

She returned to Manchester this time to the Ducie Arms, Strangeways, and studied at the School of Art under its headmaster and Academician William Muckley before taking off again to Paris and Rome.

St Ann's Square, Manchester, painted in 1910 by Elizabeth Chapman, Academy Treasurer from 1923 to 1938

She was one of the original women members of the Academy and in the 1880s founded the Manchester Women's Painters Society with Annie Swynnerton, playing an active role in both, even after moving to London in 1904.

She painted portraits, many of children, but also produced jewel-like landscapes of France and Italy. Work in the exhibition of 1927 included *Italian Women in Church* which was purchased by her friends for the city's collection.

Francis Dodd's fledgling career was encouraged by C.P. Scott, the editor of the *Manchester Guardian*, and Joseph Knight, the head of Bury Art School, who introduced him to Isabel

Dacre. Thirty years his senior, she became his friend and mentor. He remained touchingly devoted from their first meeting until she died and painted several beautiful portraits of her, including the *Signora Lotto* in Manchester Art Gallery.

They lived in the house she shared with Florence Monkhouse at 10 South King Street, later moving to 10 Acomb Street near Whitworth Park. The large house and studio, christened The Red Elephant's Castle, soon became a meeting place for the artistic community. Eva Noar, the miniaturist painter, recalled the painting sessions and exhibitions held there and how Francis with his sparkling wit and wicked sense of humour enjoyed it all. His brother-in-law, Muirhead Bone, and Henry Lamb, a friend so inspired by it all that he abandoned his study of medicine to become an artist, painted there. Both Dodd and Lamb were later elected Royal Academicians.

In 1904, the year Francis and Isabel left Acomb Street for London, he became a member of

Academy members working from the figure at the Acomb Street studio the New English Art Club. He also fell in love with Mai Ingle. Her father would not allow them to marry until Francis was earning £1,000 a year. It took seven years of hard work and determination before he was eligible, and they married, but she proved to be a cold and forbidding woman.

Both Francis and Isabel maintained an active role in the Manchester Academy while pursuing successful careers in London. He was President from 1920 to 1923, and kept other links with the North, writing for the *Manchester Guardian* under the initials P.I. for Pictor Ignotus. There was an affectionate bond with the city, reflected in his words, 'There are times when the mist of Manchester is as soft and caressing to the eye as the colour of a dove's wing, and the lights in the streets gleam like opal.'

Number 10 Acomb Street became a shirt factory, but not for long. It was to play an even more important part in the life of the Academy when it became the family home and studio of the Bancroft family. They moved in in 1906. When Elias Bancroft retired in 1922 and his wife, Louisa, became Secretary, she threw open the studio for Academy classes. For the next twenty-six years it was a base for both students and Academicians. There were regular exhibitions of members' work, and under Bertram Nicholls, a driving force in the educational aspect of the Academy, life classes were held several times a week. After Louisa retired in 1938 the Academy bought the property, and it was a centre of activities and the home of the incumbent secretary until 1948. The house was bombed in the blitz and the cost of repair was prohibitive. The once affluent area was in decline and the new secretary had no wish to live there. The house was sold and students transferred to the Midday Studios run by Margo Ingham in Mosley Street until 1951, then to the Regional College of Art until 1955, when classes were discontinued.

CHAPTER 6

The 1930s

During the 1930s the deaths of several Academicians marked the end of an era. Past President Tom Mostyn died in 1930. He had studied at Herkomer's school in Bushy, and was a member of the Royal Cambrian Academy and the Royal Society of British Artists. His rather traditional portraits contrasted with his imaginative landscapes full of 'blazing colour', but the paintings of religious subjects were most popular: 50,000 came to see his *Gethsemane* when Agnews exhibited it at the City Art Gallery. He had died relatively young compared with other Academicians: ninety-three-year-old Houghton Hague from Oldham, had been a member for sixty-one years. As a teacher at the Lyceum in his home town he inspired many pupils including Academicians William Stott of Oldham and Frederick Jackson from Middleton. Byron Cooper, known as the moonlight painter, died. He had exhibited annually at the Royal Academy for fifty-two years and held twice-yearly shows at his studio in the Royal Exchange.

Other people who reached the end of long and active lives included Gertrude Wright, a sculptor known for her small-scale figures, Isabel Dacre, Annie Swynnerton, Fanny Sugars, who was passionate about the hills and moors and whose sensitive portrait of her mother is in the collection of the Manchester Art Gallery, and Emma Magnus. The latter remains the longest-serving Literary Secretary or Archivist of the Academy.

Radical changes which would redefine the Manchester Academy occurred in 1931.

Under the direction of the President, Bertram Nicholls, the Constitution was revised and the rules altered so that any member of the public living or having lived within a twenty-five-mile radius of the Town Hall could submit work for inclusion in the Annual Spring Exhibition. The Chairman and Deputy Chairman of the City Art Gallery Committee were co-opted on to the Academy Council and Selection Panel. Associate membership was to be abolished with the gradual absorption of successful candidates into full membership.

It was hoped that the inclusion of non-members' work would increase the vitality of the Academy and encourage a wider range of artists to apply for membership. The *Manchester Evening News* echoed expectations that the developments would 'result in a representative exhibition worthy of the best tradition of Manchester as an art centre'. The resulting success of the 1932 show set the pattern for the future.

Within four years sixteen new members were voted in: Ethel Gabain and John Copley, Emmanuel Levy, Harry Rutherford and L.S. Lowry were elected, and cotton tycoons who painted

L.S. Lowry,
*An Organ
Grinder.*
Courtesy of
Manchester
Art Gallery

for pleasure such as James Chettle, Maxwell Reekie and Forrest Hewitt joined, bringing their business acumen with them. Over the next four years Associates were phased out and the twenty-five-mile radius stipulation was relaxed, although most artists had or claimed to have Manchester connections. The *Observer* critic wrote: 'Manchester Academy of Fine Arts continues its policy of welcoming work by non-members and the result is to everyone's advantage.'

The Great Depression of the 1930s did not have a catastrophic effect in Manchester which had developed its great engineering and chemical industries, but the 'economic storm' referred to at an AGM was causing hardship. During this period several Academicians were based in London, but the links with Manchester remained strong; work was exhibited at the Spring Exhibition, and in 1934 the first reunion dinner to bring together Academy members was held at Kettner's Restaurant in Soho; these dinners were held on the evening before the Royal Academy opening almost every year until 1951, when they transferred to the Manchester City Art Gallery.

One artist firmly rooted in the north was L.S. Lowry. His work was singled out from the beginning. The *Manchester Guardian* critic observed 'Mr Lowry sees his Lancashire with the intensity of an Italian primitive... he paints chimneys as Lorenzo Monaco painted saints. Their black forms rise like threatening spears from a grey landscape.' Between 1937 and 1972 Lowry exhibited over fifty paintings at the Annual Academy Exhibitions. They included *Crime Lake* in 1945, *Peel Park* and *Good Friday, Daisy Nook* in 1949, and *Piccadilly Gardens* in 1955. Paintings of single figures included *A Half Witted Child* in 1938, *Portrait of a Firewatcher* in 1944, *Man Drinking a Cup of Water* and *Man Lying at the Foot of Stairs* in 1963 and *A Young Man* in 1970.

Large companies began to commission work: the sculptor, Alan Brough, was asked to make two busts of a Lancashire man and woman for Manchester Collieries Ltd using coal. He had difficulty mastering the technique of handling it, but said the chippings came in useful.

When Manchester City won the Cup Final in 1934 the event was painted by Charles Cundall, who later recorded the coronation of George VI. The painting, *Coronation Day* was bought by Queen Mary, mother of the new King.

Stirrings of unease ran under normal life. By 1937 people were praying for peace. A few months later the *Manchester Guardian* recorded meagre sales at the Academy, blaming uncertain times and noting that the art market was a sensitive barometer of economic conditions.

Although the threat of war was looming the exhibition in the Spring of 1939 did not reflect it; the *Manchester Evening News* reported the Private View as usual, noting the sartorial dress, the new spring hats, the pin-striped suits and red ties. Members travelled to London for the annual dinner where speakers included John Rothenstein, Director of the Tate Gallery, and Margaret Pilkington and Lawrence Haward from Manchester.

James Chettle, *War Memorial*. Courtesy of Manchester Art Gallery
The view from Abingdon Street looking across Portland Street and up Major Street towards the Grand Hotel.
Chettle wrote, 'I have tried to express more than a mere record of ruined buildings … is it too much to hope
that no further subjects of the same kind will be presented to us?'

CHAPTER 7

1939 to 1945

War was declared in September. In October the *Manchester Guardian* reported that the Art Gallery intended to maintain normal services to the fullest extent that conditions would allow, and that the Manchester Academy was to hold its usual Spring Exhibition. Lawrence Haward, speaking at the opening of the 1942 exhibition recalled how, as Curator of the City Art Gallery, he had immediately phoned the Chairman of the Council at the outbreak of the war and said, 'I assume you agree with me we don't close at any cost?' He believed that it was precisely because of war that contacts with art were necessary.

Officially art was referred to as 'non essential', but the Government was not caught on the hop as it had been in 1914. Official war artists were immediately appointed, and as early as 1940 the Artists' Advisory Committee to the Ministry of Information had organised an exhibition at the National Gallery.

There was little evidence of the war in the Academy exhibitions. With the odd exception such as Ethel Gabain's *Decontaminating Gas Masks*, landscapes of picturesque streams and hills were in the majority. This form of idealistic escapism was reflected in other art forms, especially cinema.

The proximity of huge chemical and engineering plants made the area a prime target for the Luftwaffe: three nights before Christmas in 1940 the blitz started. Incendiary bombs hit Portland Street, Mosley Street and Piccadilly. Miraculously the Art Gallery survived. In the annual report it was recorded that 'Although three galleries narrowly escaped being bombed [there was] very slight damage by enemy action'. In fact the nearby blazing warehouses burnt out of control, lighting the sky for miles around. The extent of the devastation is evident in *War Memorial*, a painting of nearby Major Street by James Chettle.

Seventy per cent of the Edwardian and Victorian buildings of the city were destroyed in the war. One of the casualties of the 1940 air raid was Cross Street Unitarian Chapel, a place of worship since 1693. Alan Brough's symbolic sculpture, *Rebirth*, carved from one of the charred beams was on view at an open air service in the ruins in 1942. The sculpture was later taken to Chowbent Chapel in Atherton for safekeeping, ironically the site for another Academician's sculpture for the millennium fifty-eight years later, before being installed in the rebuilt Chapel.

The exhibition by official war artists at the City Art Gallery in 1941 included work by Nash, Sutherland, Pitchforth and several Academicians: Cundall, tackling his usual documentary subjects,

Ethel Gabain, *The Weaver* [lithograph] in the mill of Richard Haworth and Co. Ltd.
Courtesy of Manchester Art Gallery

Alan Brough, *Rebirth*. Courtesy of Cross Street Chapel, Manchester

painted Spitfires under construction at A.V. Roe's in Chadderton, portraits by Lamb and Dugdale were alongside Dodd's munition workers and Ethel Gabain painted evacuees. Perhaps it was the influence of this exhibition that led the *Manchester Guardian*, reporting on the Annual Academy show of the following year, to observe that 'The most significant feature is the interest which some of the artists are beginning to take in the aesthetic aspects of a world at war... L.S. Lowry's *Street Scene* hurts like a broken tooth... John Copley's *Destruction* makes grey-faced figures beside a tangled mass of wreckage movingly expressive [there is] a bitter sense of unreason.' Perhaps it was simply the immediacy of the war which demanded a response.

Although difficulties in obtaining materials for painting and sculpture resulted in work of smaller proportions, and some work intended for exhibition was lost in the blitz, by 1943 the Academy Exhibition was said by the *Manchester Guardian* to have 'triumphed over circumstances to the extent of getting together a show of peacetime size'.

Before his retirement after thirty-one years as Curator of the City Art Gallery Lawrence Haward organised a record in paint of Manchester's wartime industry. He asked individual firms to commission artists of his choice to paint 'workers on the home front' and to donate the results to the City. Most of the artists had Mancunian connections and included Academicians Clause, Cundall, Dodd, Gabain, Grimmond, Hagedorn, Lamb, Schwabe and Workman. They were let loose in cotton mills making uniform and camouflage, Vickers Armstrong making guns and torpedoes, A.V. Roe making Lancaster bombers, Dunlop making barrage balloons, and the great engineering firm of Metropolitan Vickers. Other firms taking part were Ferranti, Ford, Pilkington and the research laboratories at ICI and the Shirley Institute.

Manchester was richer in artistic terms because of Haward's influence, yet the proposal to mark his retirement with the purchase of his portrait by Henry Lamb was blocked by the Council, watchful, as usual, on its purse strings. Luckily Margaret Pilkington organised a colletion to buy the painting for the City's permanent collection. It was a fitting tribute by the woman, who as Honorary Director of the Whitworth Art Gallery and member of the Academy, had often worked alongside Lawrence Haward.

Thomas Dugdale, *Wartime Scene*

The large headline in January 1946 in the *Manchester Evening News* 'Artists in Evening Dress Again' symbolised the feeling of euphoria in post-war Britain. The blackout which had put a stop to many social occasions after dark was over. The conversazione was reinstated: academic robes, uniform or tails for the gentlemen were de rigueur, ladies wore long gowns and an orchestra played. When the City's permanent exhibition reopened a red carpet was laid out on the gallery steps.

Ethel Gabain, *Cathode Ray Tubes*. Courtesy of Manchester Art Gallery

Theodore Major, *Wigan Street*. Courtesy of Dr Mary Major

CHAPTER 8

1945 to 1960

The post-war period was a time of paradox: the Arts, especially theatre and cinema, still reflected escapism from austerity, the 'feel good factor' was positively encouraged and in painting English Post-Impressionism was still prevalent. The Academy was castigated for 'middle class escapism' and 'humdrum banality', but alongside the safe familiar formats the

Portrait of Margo Ingham by Ian Grant. Courtesy of Manchester Art Gallery

work of artists trying to get to grips with contemporary life and landscape was emerging.

A strong base had been established before the war by L.S. Lowry, Emmanuel Levy, Harry Rutherford, Karl Hagedorn and Harold Workman. They were joined in the 1940s by Terry McGlynn, Ian Grant, Delia Massey and Hal Yates, and the 1950s heralded an influx of more members – people of the calibre of Theodore Major, Brian Bradshaw, Norman Jaques, Richard Weisbrod, Roger Hampson and Edith Le Breton. The powerful direct response of these artists to the life and landscape they experienced established a Northern School of Painting. Alan Lowndes and William Turner were part of the School and were regular exhibitors although the former was not a member and the latter did not become an Academician until 1980.

Within the work of these and other members of the Academy were diverse strands: Hal Yates' conventional watercolours were poles apart from Major's stark treatment of the Wigan landscape. Edith Le Breton's interpretation of her Altrincham neighbourhood bore no relation to Leeds-based Owen Bowen's paintings of the Yorkshire Dales. The bold work of Bradshaw contrasted with Robert Tuson's exquisite still lifes. Excellence of technique was no longer the ultimate aim of many Academicians; Terry McGlynn was experimenting with oil and watercolour in the same painting and using newspaper prints as part of the design in his work, while the strength of the honest, forthright approach to the subject was typical of the Northern School.

In 1947 Ned Owens stood for several hours in the rain outside the City Art Gallery handing out leaflets to artists submitting work to the Academy Exhibition. He was offering them the chance to exhibit rejected work at the Midday Studios, which had recently been opened by his wife, Margo Ingham, across the road in Mosley Street under a shoe shop. There had been rumbling criticism of the Academy by frustrated modernist painters who thought it was run by influential people 'only dabbling in painting' and giving preference to purely traditional work. The ensuing exhibition at the Midday Studios proved to be a lacklustre disappointment full of second-rate work, but a Salon des Refusés had been established which became a popular and controversial 'alternative' event, transferring for a few years in the later 50s across the road to Gibb's bookshop and resurfacing for a time in the late 70s.

In 1948 one of the 'dabblers' who had refuted Ned Owens' allegations, Maxwell Reekie, died. His obituary and that of Randolph Schwabe, who died around the same time highlight the two traditions from which Academicians in the early 30s had been drawn. Reekie was typical of the wealthy, often philanthropic, businessmen who painted in an amateur capacity. Educated at Manchester Grammar School and Owens College, he was the director of the textile firm, Robert Barbour and Bro. The only formal art training he received was at evening classes run for a period in Manchester by Sickert. He was a Director of the Atheneum Club and member of its Graphic Club and President of the RMI. He was a Liberal, a member of the Reform Club and elder of

William Turner, *St Mary's Stockport*

the Presbyterian church in Didsbury.

Randolph Schwabe NEAC was typical of the majority of Academicians of the time. Born in Manchester in 1885, he had followed the familiar path to the Slade and Academie Julien in Paris after studying in Manchester. He was a watercolourist, draughtsman, etcher and lithographer, a 'genial debonair Bohemian' to be seen strolling with his dark cloak, tall hat and ivory-knobbed cane. Following the trend of several artists he moved to London, but continued to take an active part in the Academy. He was drawing master at the Royal College of Art and became Henry Tonks' successor at the Slade.

Ian Grant, Head of Painting at the Manchester College of Art, had encouraged Margo Ingham in her venture to open the Midday Studios. He held the first one-man show there in 1947, followed by L.S. Lowry in 1948. There were twice yearly exhibitions which sometimes transferred to London galleries by painters of the Northern School, often known as the Manchester Group. Academicians including Terry McGlynn, Ian Grant, John Bold, Theodore Major, Richard Weisbrod, Jose Christopherson, Ned Owens and Ronald Allan, the latter described as the last of the Manchester Bohemians, were regular contributors. Norman Jaques recalls the sheer energy and enthusiasm of Margo Ingham, and her confidence in the progress of contemporary art in the region.

The lease on the building was suddenly terminated in 1951. The news of the imminent closure was broken at a party celebrating the gallery's Festival of Britain Exhibition. New premises were never found for the Midday Studios which had played such a vital role promoting the work of northern artists.

Manchester was cushioned from the worst effects of the collapse of the cotton industry in the 1950s by the existence of some of the industries which had attracted bombing raids a few years earlier. Fewer members found it necessary to be based in London. Various factors contributed to the shift including the fact that the Royal Academy and a handful of dealers within one square mile of the West End no longer had a stranglehold on sales opportunities. In the early 1960s there were over a hundred private galleries spreading outwards from the centre of London, and the upsurge in the number of galleries willing to promote and 'nurse' artists influenced the market.

James Fitton, *Tavern Brawl*. Courtesy of Gallery Oldham

The opening up of artistic channels worked both ways: contemporary work not seen often since the great exhibitions of the RMI and of Agnew's was once again easily available to the people of the North-West. The recently formed Arts Council was responsible for bringing major exhibitions of work by Picasso and Henry Moore to the City Art Gallery. The Festival of Britain Exhibition 'Sixty Painters for 1951' featured the work of artists including L.S. Lowry, Ruskin Spear, Ivon Hitchens, Patrick Heron and Matthew Smith. This cutting edge of modernism excited controversy, not least in the Corporation Council Chamber where after a debate described by the Chairman as a 'violent and jeering diatribe' councillors voted eighty-four to twenty against spending £500 on the 'freak of imagination' *Still Life 1950* by Ben Nicholson.

In 1949 the Crane Gallery opened in a basement formerly a white-tiled air raid shelter at 35 South King Street. Paintings and sculpture by London-based artists like Muirhead Bone, Michael Rothenstein and Carel Weight were for sale. Some Academicians who exhibited there included Theodore Major and Brian Bradshaw who had a joint show in 1958.

The title of the Academy exhibition was changed in 1952 from the Spring Exhibition to the Annual Exhibition; an appropriate if belated renaming as it had been held in January for some time. The *Manchester Guardian* noted that the gesture seemed symbolic of a deeper change with less slick, more powerful work from people like Harold Workman and John Bold, Delia Massey and Janet Kirk. Terry McGlynn's *Port Vendres* was deemed his 'most considerable work yet produced' and Theodore Major 'breaks new ground with his *Crucifixion*'. Willett wrote of Ian Grant: 'Nowhere else in this show is colour so subtly and satisfyingly handled as in his *Disley Woods, November*, or his admirable portrait of red haired Miss Margaret Gumuchian.'

The custom of holding Autumn exhibitions of members' work, popular events at Acomb Street until the property was sold in 1948, was continued the following year with an exhibition of watercolours at the Whitworth Art Gallery. A policy of taking work out to Northern towns resulted in shows at Rochdale Art Gallery in 1950, Oldham Art Gallery in 1951, Bury Art Gallery in 1952 and Bradford's Cartwright Hall in 1955. Members were represented in other exhibitions around this time: the Festival of Britain Exhibition at Salford Art Gallery, 'The Lancashire Scene', was a showcase for the Northern School of Artists.

Exhibitions at the City Art Gallery of paintings, prints and sculpture by the staff of the Regional College of Art included the work of several Academy members. Continuous links between the College and the Academy have existed since the 1850s when the headmaster, James Hammersley, was instrumental in creating the Academy. Originally the School of Design, then the School of Art, it moved from the Mosely Street building to Cavendish Street in 1882. Ten years later it was taken over by the City and became the Municipal School of Art. Many Academicians have studied and taught there and in 1955 John Holden was the third Principal to be elected a member. When the School became the Regional College of Art, Norman Jaques recalls Holden reorganising courses to adopt a progressive approach to art training. The relationship has continued through subsequent years to the present time. In 1970 the College amalgamated with others to become the Manchester Polytechnic, and in 1992 it assumed University status as part of the Manchester Metropolitan University.

In 1951 John Gauld became President. The same year three Honorary Members were elected: Sir Hubert Worthington, planning

Terry McGlynn discussing one of his paintings

consultant to the University, and College of Science and Technology, and architect in charge of restoring many buildings in the city after bomb damage, James Fitton RA, a modernist painter from Oldham, and Sir Winston Churchill. Ironically it had been Churchill who had encouraged his pal, Sir Alfred Munnings, to hold the Royal Academy banquet a couple of years previously at which he had delivered the infamous tirade against Modern Art, and in 1956 James Fitton became the object of Munnings' antipathy when he was one of the two main contestants to take over the RA Presidency. Munnings, who supported the traditionalist Charles Wheeler, dragged himself out of convalescence to vote declaring, 'I had to come. I heard that creature Fitton might be elected.'

Industrial Lancashire with its sulphurous 'smogs' and black encrusted buildings was the subject of a growing number of artists. The scenery of Wigan, Bolton, Hyde, Manchester, Salford and Stockport was tackled alongside the more 'picturesque' mountains and waterfalls. Some critics were patronisingly dismissive of the latter, but it was the treatment of these subjects, typical of a seam of technically good but derivative work running through the exhibitions which caused offence. This was the era of weekend migration from the closed-in streets to the new National Parks, four of which were within easy reach of Manchester. Areas of great natural beauty were increasingly relevant to the lives of the general public.

L.S. Lowry, *The Cripples*, exhibited at Manchester Academy in 1955. © The Lowry Collection, Salford

Terry McGlynn was one of several artists who challenged accepted values; he had studied in Manchester and Paris where he came under the influence of Abstract Expressionism. He emphasised the creative rather than the representational aspect of a painting, and held annual exhibitions at his studio in Heaton Mersey, Stockport, which won critical acclaim. In 1954 Alan Sewter of the *Manchester Guardian*, husband of future Academician Margarita Medina, wrote, 'Mr. McGlynn is something of a magician... we are positively bewitched'.

At this period there was a lively use of watercolour as a medium with a strong and sometimes experimental element in freely handled gouaches, and the quality of printmaking and drawing, not so apparent since the wood engravings and etchings of wildlife by Charles Tunnicliffe in the 1930s and 1940s, was prominent. Powerful drawing also figured in work exploring more unusual subjects. Brian Bradshaw's painting of a 'tumbled and unmade bed' was praised by Alan Sewter for the 'tautness of its linear patterns'.

In 1956 Ned Owens was asked to make a series of drawings recording the construction of Lark Hill Place, the nineteenth-century street at Salford Art Gallery. The Director responsible, Albert Frape, was the man who built up Britain's largest collection of the work of L.S. Lowry at the gallery.

The portrayal of the human figure reflected the differences in approach. The excellent conventional portraits of friends and established dignitaries by Gladys Vasey and Frederick Deane, himself a distinctive figure with his eye patch a permanent reminder of the eye lost at Arnhem, contrasted with the stark shock of Lowry's *Cripples* and *Funeral Party*.

Observations of people in daily life were lifted from the mundane by Hampson's *Domino Players* and *Lacemaker*, Levy's *Landlord* and *Girl in a Doorway* and *Les Girls* by James Fitton. The two figures in Derek Wilkinson's *The Beach* 'will cause a sensation' the critic of the *Evening Chronicle* reported, going on to explain : [the painting] 'shows a couple, the man in a lounge suit, the girl in a skirt and jumper lying on the deserted beach locked in each others arms'.

The year was 1959. The public was innocently unaware that it was about to enter the maelstrom of the swinging sixties.

The climax of celebrations to mark the Academy's centenary was a dinner at the Town Hall attended by over two hundred and fifty people and set against the backdrop of Ford Madox Brown's murals. The guest speakers were Sir Philip Hendy, Director of the National Gallery, and Trenchard Cox, Director of the Victoria and Albert Museum, who spoke of his admiration for the Academy in giving artists who had talent a chance to show their work and establish a reputation. He said that work done by the Academy in collaboration with the City Art Gallery 'brings to museums the essential living quality which is the lifeblood of these institutions'.

That year the annual exhibition, which ran for the usual five weeks and attracted almost 18,000 visitors, was partly retrospective. Works by successive Academicians from the Victorian artists to contemporary painters and sculptors could be seen at the same time. They included William Percy's portrait of his friend, the writer Edwin Waugh, Ford Madox Brown's epic painting, *Work*, Francis Dodd's *Signora Lotto*, *Lamorna* by Lamorna Birch, Chettle's stark blitz painting, Levy's *Yellow Clown* and Lowry's *Onlookers*. Alan Sewter could report in the *Manchester*

Guardian, [the Academy] 'has successfully weathered many storms and is still ship shape enough to face with some confidence the voyages ahead of it'.

A booklet outlining the first hundred years of the Academy compiled by the Literary Secretary, Hal Yates, was published to mark the occasion.

The Centenary Exhibition had only six free-standing sculptures: Joseph Swynnerton's *The Offering*, John Cassidy's bust of Clarence Whaite, *Figure With Bird* by new member, William Bailey and three pieces, *Cosmopolitan Head*, *Family Group* and *War Group* by a sculptor elected the previous year. His name was Edward Roocroft.

Ted Roocroft was a farmer's son from Eccleston near Chorley. His career in

Ted Roocroft [centre] delivering his work for the annual exhibition helped by a gallery attendant [left] and Ian Thompson [right], one of his students and future MAFA President. (Photograph: *Manchester Evening News*)

sculpture began almost by chance. After escaping from Dunkirk in the war, Private Roocroft was stationed in Edinburgh where he took up 'whittling', carving a wooden horse for his daughter, Olive. His work drew the attention of the Commanding Officer who sent him to classes at the Edinburgh College of Art. Back in 'civvy street' he enquired about further training, but the rehabilitation officer was not sympathetic. As Ted said later, 'If you wasn't studying before the war, you hadn't a hope in hell.' He became a labourer, but continued to carve and soon got the chance to study with the help of Preston's Director of Education. After a year at Manchester, he went to the Slade, where he was taught by Henry Moore. In the early 50s he returned north to lecture at Manchester College of Art in the sculpture school, or madhouse as he affectionately called it, where he inspired a whole generation of sculptors. His own work would gain national recognition.

In 1959 the *Manchester Guardian* changed its name to *The Guardian*. From 1961 it was printed in London, and three years later the editor moved south. The close ties which had existed between the historic newspaper and the Academy for over a hundred years were loosened.

Artists had not had many opportunities to exhibit their work in private galleries in the city centre since the closure of the Midday Studios, although Gibb's bookshop had been a venue for intermittent exhibitions since 1934. A sculptor whose work was shown there, Geoffrey Green, opened a gallery in Tib Lane in June 1959. In the 60s Academicians including Harold Riley, Derek Wilkinson, Jose Christopherson, Margarita Medina, Terry McGlynn and Roger Hampson had exhibitions there. Future members like William Turner, Brian Nolan and John McCombs also had shows. The gallery, run by Geoffrey's wife, Jan, exhibited the work of a succession of members over the next four decades, and continues to be a venue for several academicians today.

Roger Hampson, *Domino Players*. Courtesy of Mrs Betty Hampson

Ted Roocroft, *Heavy Sow*, holly wood 1982. Collection of Don McKinlay

CHAPTER 9

The 1960s

The first decade after the centenary was epitomised by the strength of the council and officers. Harry Rutherford took over as President after the death of John Gauld in 1961. Harold Williamson was both Vice-President and Treasurer, Donald Rayner was Secretary and Hal Yates Literary Secretary. Kenneth Clark, William Coldstream and Geoffrey Parkes were Trustees and Anne Redpath was elected Honorary Member. Winston Churchill had been Honorary Vice-President since 1952.

The Council of 1963 included Iola Spafford, Derek Wilkinson, Norman Jaques and Roger Hampson who were joined on the selection panel by Wilfred Wood, Fred Deane, Ian Grant, Terry McGlynn and George L. Conran, Curator of the City Art Gallery. This team was responsible for the exhibition held over five weeks in the notoriously bitter winter of 1964. The blizzards may have explained the drop in visitors from the average 12,000 to just over 9,000, but otherwise statistics were typical of annual exhibitions. Out of almost 1,000 submissions two hundred and forty were selected and double hung in four of the first-floor galleries.

Three functions took place at the start of the show; the original soirée which ladies could attend had years ago changed its name to the equally romantic conversazione, an evening event for artists, subscribers and friends. In 1904 Varnishing Day had become the Preview, held in the afternoon, and the dinner with special guest speakers inaugurated as a reunion in London for members based in the North and South was now held at the Art Gallery.

The method of electing members had changed little over the years, although the annual subscription had risen to three guineas. Membership was open to painters, sculptors, engravers and architects nominated by two Academicians and on submission of specimens of their work approved by the Council at a special meeting. Edward Salomons, a Fellow of the Royal Institute of Architects, had wryly observed in 1859 that it would be difficult to present a building; the acceptance of plans and drawings solved the problem.

The influx of new members in the early 60s included Harold Riley, Margaret Gumuchian, Morgan Hewinson, and Peter Shaw. Josef Herman was made an honorary member. Because the annual exhibition was open to all, artists not necessarily wanting to be members such as Margo Ingham and Leonard McComb submitted paintings. Norman Adams, later elected Honorary member, sent work in, and future Academicians Irene Halliday and Brian Nolan, at the beginning of their careers, had the opportunity to exhibit.

Three-dimensional work assumed an increasingly high profile. Ted Roocroft was establishing a national reputation particularly as sculptor of animals. He kept pigs at his smallholding near Knutsford, and pigs in concrete, pigs in bronze, in slate, marble and wood were his trademark. Sheep made good subjects and orang-utans and the human figure, carved with a strength and sensitivity apparent in the series of cosmopolitan groups symbolising unity of nations through a cosmopolitan growth. He had a close affinity with organic life, and a plentiful supply of holly, laburnum, sycamore, damson, elm, beech and ash in the Cheshire countryside meant he could eye up a living tree or a fallen log for years before starting to reveal the form within it.

Harry Rutherford was President from 1961 to 1969, a period of massive social change when youth culture invaded the mainstream. It was the era of the Beatles, Elvis and sexual liberation. Even the BBC broadcast outrageous satire. Far-reaching changes in art education caused a

Harry Rutherford, *Mill Girls, Ashton*. Courtesy of Astley Cheetham Art Collection, Tameside MBC and Mrs Mary Fielder

furore in some quarters. Ted Roocroft believed 'creative ability and technique of the highest order' were both necessary and one without the other was fatal. Twenty years later he said, 'In the sixties they threw technique out of the window... the things you could teach were neglected so you did get in a helluva mess'.

Art and opinions about art were open to all interpretations; critics lurched too far in support or condemnation, often tripping themselves up in the process. Rutherford's observation made in 1963 'In

Roger Hampson, *Miners*. Courtesy of Jan Green of Tib Lane Gallery and Mrs Betty Hampson

these days of supersonic speed, of reaching for the moon... space travel has one thing in common with one sort of contemporary art – monkeys are capable of both', was borne out a few months later when a critic writing about a painting by 'Pierre Brassau' claimed, 'Every touch of the brush is thoroughly calculated. His technique is marked by an almost violent sumptuousness.' It was the work of Peter, the chimpanzee, with a liking for cobalt blue.

Rutherford showed astute appraisal of the situation in comments made in 1967: [it is] 'fruitless to disregard new movements. Vitality matters... from the very shock of ideas in this day and age the light will shine... all progress comes from a clash of cultures.'

Harry Rutherford was born in Denton in 1903 and studied under Valette. He was greatly influenced by Sickert who had opened classes in Manchester in 1925 at the request of Jackson, the art dealer. After travels in Europe, Rutherford ended up in London, penniless, hanging round Fleet Street for freelance work. He was lucky; in 1937 he got a regular job sketching 'live' on BBC TV at Alexandra Palace. He became a pioneer television personality, drawing stars as they performed until war closed down television. Afterwards he resumed broadcasting with his own children's sketchbook series. He was a prominent member of the Chelsea Arts Club for forty years, and an exhibitor at the Royal Academy for thirty years. In the early 1950s he returned north to live in Hyde, and lectured at Manchester Regional College of Art from 1952 to 1969. His powerful paintings recording the contemporary life and landscape of the region are of national significance, and he remains one of the most influential artists of the period.

In 1963 it was reported that there were plans to demolish the Atheneum. The building, next door to the Art Gallery and designed by the same architect, Sir Charles Barry, had been bought by the City Council in 1938 in order to extend the gallery, but this was shelved because of the war. Land had already been acquired adjacent to the gallery, and at an estimated cost of £1million an extension was planned incorporating the site of the Atheneum. Luckily the plans were never realised; yet again development was in abeyance.

Almost from the time the RMI had handed over the building, space to house the growing permanent collection of art had been at a premium. Between 1910 and 1935 there had been a series of complex proposals to build a new gallery in Piccadilly. The Corporation had bought the site when the Infirmary moved in 1904, but the schemes, held up by the First World War, never came to fruition. An eventual decision was made to create an open space on the site, and Piccadilly Gardens were created. Lawrence Haward commissioned Lowry to make a series of sketches of the gardens in the 1930s.

In the late 60s a business man, Alan Behar, thought of opening up the basement of a textile company in Portland Street as a gallery. He was recommended by Margo Ingham to approach Colin Jellicoe, an artist running a gallery with Geoffrey Key in Rusholme. A business partnership was formed and the Colin Jellicoe Gallery opened in 1968, giving more members of the Academy opportunities to exhibit their work in a private gallery in the city centre.

The following year Roger Hampson became President. His uncompromising portrayals of millworkers, miners and collieries had established him as a prominent painter and printmaker and his work was admired by Lowry, who bought several pieces from Hampson's exhibition at Salford Art Gallery.

He continued the Academy's policy of encouraging young artists, fostering links with local art schools. Life classes for students had transferred to and gradually been absorbed by the Art College after the closure of the Midday Studios, but prizes for work exhibited by students continued. The money came from the interest on the bequest of £500 made in 1884 by Mrs E. Salisbury Heywood. The Northern Arts Foundation, later the Granada Foundation, topped up the prize money in 1969 with an annual grant, so it was possible to award £200 to artists under thirty years old for work of outstanding merit in the Open Exhibition.

L.S. Lowry and Ellis Shaw, 1971. Courtesy of the *Oldham Evening Chronicle*

CHAPTER 10

The 1970s and 1980s

Geoffrey Key was one of the first artists to win a popular 'under thirty' award in 1971 with paintings of Salford. Another young member concerned with Salford subject matter, Harold Riley, was influenced by Lowry and helped by the Academy stalwart, Hal Yates, whose encouragement, said Riley, had a 'predominant effect' on his own work. He was commissioned by Salford University to make a portrait of its Chancellor, Prince Philip. The painting, exhibited first at Salford Art Gallery and in 1974 at the Academy, departed from the traditional, showing the Prince in a brown lounge suit with the ceremonial robes draped on a table behind him.

In 1972 Carol Kroch of the *Daily Telegraph* noted, 'New blood gives Academy a lift', and the following year Jane Clifford, writing for the same newspaper, praised the work of Harry Rutherford, John Bold, Iola Spafford and the large abstract painting *Gannets* by Norman Adams, an honorary member since 1968 and Head of Painting at Manchester Polytechnic.

The sending in of increasingly large canvases was becoming a problem: the non-members' hanging fee of £1 was adjusted to payment by size – £1 for up to 5 ft, £1.50 for 5ft to 10ft, and £3 for 10ft to a maximum of 15ft.

As part of the Manchester Festival of 1973 the Academy staged an exhibition of members' work, borrowed from the City Art Gallery's collection, at the Renold Building, UMIST. Sir Tom Monnington, President of the RA, opened the show which was accompanied by a display of photographs and documents from the archives, and an updated version of Hal Yates' booklet which had been produced for the centenary.

The honest individual work of the Northern School continued to flourish. *Guardian* critic, Merete Bates, admired Roger Hampson's *Miners* and *Street Musicians*, Norman Jaques' *Landscape with Lake* and Arthur Delaney's *Mill Street, Ancoats*. The latter was not an Academician, but in common with other established artists often sent work into the Open Exhibitions. John McCombs, a future member who had been inspired by the annual MAFA shows since he was a small boy, and had recently returned north after studying at St Martin's in London, sent work in to the exhibition for the first time.

In 1974 there were one hundred and thirty-four works by members, and one hundred and four by non-members. There was an all time sales record of £2,367, beating the previous record of 1873, but Jane Clifford writing in the *Daily Telegraph* was not impressed: she declared it to be a 'top heavy show... once again Manchester Academy has taken over half the City Art Gallery for its Annual Exhibition...'.

During the mid 70s to eighties there were contributions from architects after a gap of thirty years, and designs in the form of architectural drawings and models were submitted. In 1980 the proposal to convert the Albert Dock warehouses in Liverpool to a Maritime Museum by Peter Shuttleworth was exhibited, and Sheppard Robson's design for the Students' Union at Manchester Polytechnic.

In 1983 the Manchester firm of Spratley and Cullearn, which had reached the last seven on the shortlist in the controversial competition to design the new extension for the National Gallery, exhibited three models and nine drawings of their proposals.

Lowry died at the age of eighty-eight in 1976. Alan Lowndes said that he had painted the people pushed and crushed by the very places they kept going, and recalled with affection visits to exhibitions and Lowry's often wry sense of humour. The gallery owner, Andreas Kalman, observed that although Lowry liked to appear untidy and shabby, 'I do not think that he had ever done a shabby thing in his life.' The number of warm tributes made Lowry's reputation as a solitary man more poignant, but he himself had said, 'Had I not been lonely I should not have seen what I did.'

Another long-standing member, the watercolourist Donald Rayner RBA RI, died in 1977. He was a textile designer for Tootal's, and had been Secretary of the Academy for twenty-one years. He exhibited regularly at the RA and the Paris Salon, and his last one-man show had been at Salford Art Gallery the previous year.

Differing opinions about the proliferation of large-scale mostly abstract paintings accepted for the open exhibitions erupted into a full scale row in 1978. Out of almost nine hundred submissions only one hundred and seventy-nine works instead of the usual two hundred plus were accepted. Hal Yates claimed that the selection committee had created an atmosphere of fury and hatred and threatened to resign. One canvas was thought only good enough for throwing things at. But Keith Godwin, the incoming President, would soon have more upheaval to contend with.

In 1978 Timothy Clifford became Director of the City Art Gallery. He undertook a major reorganisation, bringing in the best of Manchester's collection from branch galleries including the Turners from Fletcher Moss and the Victorian masterpieces from Queen's Park to the City Art Gallery. 'I want to make my gallery sing', he told John Robert-Blunn of the *Manchester Evening News*, 'I want it to be ravishing'.

The logistics of rehanging these paintings to accommodate temporary exhibitions made it impractical for the Academy exhibition to be housed in the usual rooms. The Annual Exhibition relocated to the Atheneum Gallery adjoining the main building on Princess Street. Dating from 1836, it had originally been a club promoting adult education. After refurbishment it was renamed the Gallery of Modern Art. The exhibition there in 1979, the first with a new director at the gallery and a new President of the Academy, was open for five weeks instead of the three weeks of the last ten years. Because the selection committee was unsure of the amount of space available there was a limitation on the size of work submitted; nothing over 5ft 6in was allowed, making for a more cohesive show and calming the simmering rows. As John Robert-Blunn reported in the *Manchester Evening News*, 'Big is not necessarily beautiful', and Jane Clifford writing in the *Daily Telegraph* observed, 'The new look at Manchester Art Gallery has extended to the Manchester Academy of Fine Arts Exhibition'.

Dawn Rowland, *Femme de Rocher*, soapstone

By the early eighties sculptors using fibreglass, resin, steel, perspex and plastic added to the increasing vibrancy of three-dimensional work. Dawn Rowland's powerful figures often symbolising the continuing chain of human life were carved in alabaster and soapstone. Glenys Latham made a strong statement with sculpture in stone and bronze, and Keith Hamlett, who had a one-man show at Salford Art Gallery in 1983, worked in ceramic.

Seated Sow in laburnum and *New Born Piglet* in copper beech were sent in to the exhibition of 1986 by Ted Roocroft together with his maquette for a four-ton life-size sculpture of three sheep. Made in reinforced concrete studded with pieces of Derbyshire limestone for fleece on a base of Coniston green slate the work was commissioned by Manchester City Council for the Castlefield site. Another public sculpture completed for the city the same year is *Doves of Peace* on Bridge Street by Academician Mike Lyons.

Norman Jaques, *Rotting Tree Stump*

A casualty of the move to the Atheneum was the annual dinner which transferred to the Piccadilly Hotel. In 1980 the final dinner, with guest speaker Alan Bowness, Director of the Tate Gallery, was held at the University. The following year the popular buffet suppers were inaugurated at the newly named Gallery of Modern Art where in a more relaxed atmosphere artists, sponsors and friends could meet and at the same time view the exhibition.

Record prize money of £1,400 which included an open award of £500 for any work of outstanding merit was introduced in 1984, the year of the 125th anniversary of the Academy. The new prize was won by Paul Critchley for a strikingly realistic self portrait.

In the spring Norman Jaques, former senior lecturer in the Faculty of Art and Design at Manchester Polytechnic, was elected President. A respected painter and printmaker, he has exhibited work in London, Edinburgh and Nebraska. In 2000 he was made a life member in

Ian Grant with an early self portrait

recognition of the significant role he has played in the Academy over a period of fifty years.

Vera Lowe was one year into her influential term as Secretary, and Philip Livesey, a chartered accountant and Partner in Charge at Coopers and Lybrand North West (now Price Waterhouse Coopers), became Treasurer in 1984. The first person to be recruited from an exclusively different profession, his knowledge of the financial world has proved invaluable, and he continues to hold the position to the present time.

Prize money spiralled. Julian Spalding, the new Director of the City Art Gallery split the £1,000 MAFA Award for best work in the show in 1986 between veteran Ian Grant for his painting *Autumn* and Brian Woods, a Rochdale college lecturer not yet elected for his work *The Builder*. By 1987 prizes totalling over £3,000 were offered by the Academy, supported by Coopers and Lybrand, and eleven sponsors from industry and commerce whose involvement in actively encouraging the thriving art scene of the region was acknowledged by Norman Jaques.

Ian Grant was an influential member of the Academy for almost sixty years. Born in Scotland in 1904, he had studied in Glasgow at the time Post-Impressionism could still provoke outrage. He recalled an incident when a reproduction of a Van Gogh painting hung in the Glasgow School of Art refectory had caused a professor to yell, 'I cannot eat with that horrible object hanging there! Take it down!'

In Paris in the 1920s Grant experienced the poverty of a struggling artist, earning money by teaching English, and 'touching up' theatrical sets, originally painted by Picasso and Braque, for Diaghilev's ballet company. He completed his studies at the Royal College of Art, then moved north to become a lecturer in Manchester at the Regional College, and later in the extra mural department of the University. He married Margaret Gumuchian, a former student and member of the Academy in 1953. His paintings gained significant recognition and his input into northern artistic life was considerable. He helped set up the Midday Studios where he organised the first Lowry exhibition in the region, and was later involved in establishing the gallery at the Cornerhouse.

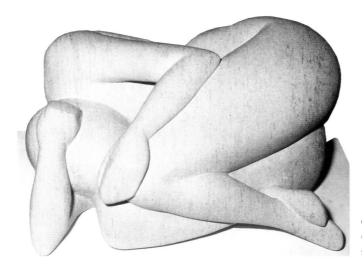

Glenys Latham, *Curled*, Ancaster stone

CHAPTER 11

The 1990s

An historic appointment was made in 1990. Glenys Latham became the first woman to be elected President of the Academy. A Bolton-based sculptor and lecturer at Leigh College of Art, she was establishing a growing reputation for her work in stone and bronze.

The influx of new members in the late eighties and early nineties added to the quality of work by long-standing members. The eclectic nature of the Academy was becoming more apparent than at any other time in its history. There were Don McKinlay's paintings of the poll tax riots, Bohuslav Barlow's surreal images of floating dogs and figures, Joseph O'Reilly's meticulous still lifes in acrylic and John Sprakes' equally perfect treatment of the same subject in tempera. There was a sculptural quality in John McCombs' paintings of the village of Delph, in Saddleworth, and Paul Critchley's unconventionally shaped canvases painted with intense brilliant colour gave a sense of looking through a keyhole. A direct response to their environment was apparent in Vera Lowe's paintings of Ramsbottom in Lancashire and George Sykes' honest portrayal of the people and places he knew around Lees, near Oldham.

By 1992 prize money had topped £6,000, and the Annual Exhibition was referred to by John Robert-Blunn in the *Manchester Evening News* as 'The most prestigious in the North for established and rising young artists', and 'The most important regional show of work by living artists'.

The Devil Pig, *The El Greco Sow* and *Resting Sheep* were exhibited by Ted Roocroft in the spring of 1991. He died in the autumn. His last piece, a ten-foot-long rhinoceros carved from a fallen elm at Arley Hall, Cheshire, was almost complete. Tributes came from many Academicians; Keith Hamlett, an ex-student and friend, expressed the appreciation felt by the people Ted had encouraged. Tom

Titherington recalled, 'All the subtlety and intelligence of his feelings towards the material and the world around him was embodied in the movement when the chisel met the wood.'

A painting in the 1993 Annual Open Exhibition exhibition, *Rhythm of the Trees*, led to headlines suggesting the selectors had been revealed with their critical trousers down. The freely executed work in poster paint on paper was by Carly Johnson, aged four. It had been submitted by her grandfather, and the novelty caught the public's imagination. The story was syndicated in newspapers around the world. There was talk of egg on faces as the selection panel had no idea of the age of the artist, but Frank Whitford, writing in the *Sunday Times*, shrewdly observed 'Almost all children are artists. They have spontaneity, energy, freshness of vision...'.

Later the same year Peter Oakley, a senior lecturer in art and design at Edgehill College, Ormskirk,

John McCombs, *Road Leading into Delph Village, Winter*

Paul Critchley, *The Balcony*

became President. A painter and printmaker gaining increasing recognition, his potent images are filled with ambiguous shapes and glowing colours. Robert Clark of the *Guardian*, in his review of Oakley's 1997 exhibition at Drumcroon Arts Centre, wrote, 'With Oakley the material world takes on the melancholic poignancy of objects left behind in hotel drawers. The passion might have passed away, but the discarded paraphernalia is still stained by the traceries of its life-affirming dynamic.'

Printmakers were becoming an increasingly strong presence by the mid nineties; a members' exhibition of prints held at Arts Intaglio on Whitworth Street West in 1994 was followed four years later by shows curated by Derek Wilkinson at the Duke's Oak Gallery, Cheshire and Stockport Art Gallery. Stan Dobbin's woodcuts,

Norman Jaques' lithographs, Julia Midgley's strangely powerful etchings and aquatints, Paul Ritchies's atmospheric etchings and Yvonne Ma's collographs headed a powerful array of linocuts, monotypes and screen-prints.

As well as taking part in the Annual MAFA Exhibition, members exhibited work independently in a widening circle rippling out from the city

Paul Ritchie, *Bass Rock*

centre. Several were with Tib Lane Gallery or the Colin Jellicoe Gallery; North-West venues included the Portico Library and Art Gallery, the public galleries of Salford and Stockport, Drumcroon Arts Centre at Wigan and the Yorkshire Sculpture Park near Wakefield.

The tradition of exhibiting at the Royal Societies based at the Mall Galleries and The Royal Academy summer exhibitions continued, but new venues in London included the Barbican, the Business Design Centre, the sculpture site at Chelsea harbour, and the National Portrait Gallery. International opportunities broadened with members showing work in Europe, America, Hong Kong, Australia, China and Japan.

Peter Oakley, *Tableau: Histories and Mysteries*

Don McKinlay, *Janina*

Sheila Dewsbury, *Above Greenfield, Saddleworth*

The introduction in 1994 of the Edward Oldham Travel Bursary gave members submitting a winning proposal a chance to work in a chosen location, producing a body of work for exhibition the following year. £1,000 awarded annually has sent artists to Venice, Barcelona, Ireland, Warsaw, the Pacific coast of North America, Nova Scotia and St Kilda.

The practice of holding regional exhibitions of members' work had been revived in 1989 with shows at the Grundy Gallery in Blackpool, and the Weaver Gallery, Weaverham, Cheshire. Others at the Brewery Arts Centre, Kendal, the Haworth Gallery, Accrington, the Atkinson Gallery, Southport, Museum Gallery, Saddleworth, the Portico Library and Gallery in Manchester and the Ashton Art Gallery followed. In 1999 David Stanley organised a show at the Quaker Gallery, London. A continuing series of these exhibitions, sometimes curated by members, sometimes by staff at the different venues, is a vibrant part of the Academy, forging links with the artistic life of the region, and exposing the work of Academicians to a wider cross-section of the public.

Irene Halliday, *Still Life, Midsummer's Night, Oban*

The last Academy Annual Open Exhibition held at the Atheneum, or Gallery of Modern Art, was in 1996. It was opened by Adrian Henri, the Liverpool poet and artist. Guest selectors included the painter, Ansel Krut, David Lee, editor of the magazine *Art Review*, and Michael Lyons, Vice-President of the Royal Society of British Sculptors, who later became a member of the Academy.

In 1997 an extended run of the David Hockney exhibition at the Atheneum led to the Annual Open Exhibition being held in the main gallery. Once more paintings, prints and sculpture by Academicians and other artists from all backgrounds whose work had survived the selection process were seen in the historic building. There were 23,906 visitors to the show which featured two hundred and thirty works representing a comprehensive range of contemporary art. Two pieces by guest selectors were sent in; Maurice Cockrill's watercolour, *E Mare Ex Industria*, and Sophie Ryder's wire sculpture, *Minotaur Head*. Members' work ranged from Linda Weir's exuberant impasto oil paintings to Irene Halliday's fresco-like gouaches, Janet Golphin's distinctive still life in acrylic to Michael Browne's pencil study of Eric Cantona and David Stanley's dream-like abstract images. Intricate paintings in a mixture of watercolour, acrylic, gouache and gold dust by twin sisters, Amrit and Rabindra Singh, combined the narrative of everyday Liverpudlian life with Persian and Mughal art. Powerful stone carvings by Dawn Rowland, Simon Manby and Danny Clahane formed part of a strong sculptural presence, and it was a nine-foot figure, *The Kirkby Kiss*, sited outside the City Art Gallery and carved from a single piece of elm by Thompson Dagnall, which won the major MAFA award of £2,000.

In the closing decade of the twentieth century there was a significant increase in work by Academicians in the public domain. Norman Adams painted the Stations of the Cross in St Mary's, the catholic church affectionately known as the Hidden Gem, in Mulberry Street, Manchester, and Peter Stanaway depicted the Stations of the Cross in a series of ceramic tiles for

St Edward's catholic church in Lees, Oldham. Ian Thompson's *Crown of Thorns* measuring almost ten feet in diameter was installed in the Parish Church of St Cross with Saint Paul, Clayton, Manchester. Michael Browne completed a commission supported by Manchester Metropolitan University and the City Council to reconstruct a replica of the Sistine Chapel on the ceiling of the Coco Too Italian Restaurant in the city centre. In 1990 Janina Cebertowicz took on the post of artist in residence at the Royal Northern College of Music, sketching students in rehearsal and on stage. An article in the *Manchester Evening News* in 1995 described her capturing the fleeting moment of a performance, 'Crouched among the stage curtains in semi-darkness, finding the crayons by touch, with a torch held between her clenched teeth'.

Thompson Dagnall, *A Kirkby Kiss*

Julia Midgley, Reader in Documentary Drawing at Liverpool John Moore's University, made 'fly on the wall' sketches of day-to-day life at the Royal Liverpool University Hospital. By chance she was on hand to record the moment fellow Academician, Peter Edge, received his brother, Stephen's, kidney in a life-saving transplant operation.

Ian Thompson, a sculptor and former student of Ted Roocroft became President in 1997. He is on the Fabric Advisory Committee for Coventry Cathedral, and has shown work in the Art in Churches exhibitions at York and Norwich Cathedrals. Mike Butler, in an article on the Academy annual exhibition, had observed, 'Ian Thompson's *Ram Caught in a Thicket* is in a long line of distinguished Academic beasts'. The Academy was about to enter one of the most critical periods of its history and, like other Presidents at such times, Ian Thompson would be required to steer it successfully through uncertain times and changing circumstances.

A massive refurbishment and extension programme at the City Art Gallery meant that it would be closed for four years from 1998. The Academy had to move to a temporary venue for

Julia Midgley, *Operation*

the Annual Open Exhibition. Janina Cebertowicz came to the rescue, offering the time slot booked for her own exhibition at Bury Art Gallery. The hospitality extended by the director, Richard Burns, and his staff made the Academy's relationship with the gallery over the next five years a memorable period. The logistics of staging the annual exhibition without the aid of the usual team of furbishers stationed at the City Art Gallery seemed formidable, but the organisational skills of the council members, and the secretary, Cliff Moorhouse, another recruit from the business sector, surmounted any difficulties.

Requests for help with mounting the show met with a huge response from members. A small army of hangers led by John McCombs dealt with the practicalities of getting the two dimensional work on the walls, and adjusting the lighting, while sculptors dealt with positioning three-dimensional pieces. Derek Wilkinson organised the sales desk, setting up a rota of people to sell work from the exhibition, catalogues, members' cards and publications. Lectures, tours of the exhibition and workshops were set up, and the addition of the Leech Award of £1,000 to the MAFA Award of £2,000 together with the continued support of sponsors meant that the prize money now topped £6,000. For the exhibition of 1998 Richard Gray, the Director of the City Art Gallery, joined the Director of Bury Art Gallery, Richard Burns, and sculptor Glyn Williams with painters John Holden and William Tillyer on the selection panel.

Sadly Vera Lowe, one of the longest serving secretaries, often referred to as 'the backbone of the Academy', died in 1998. The number of Academy affairs she organised, added to the amount of paperwork she tackled, mostly on an old typewriter, while still maintaining the quality of her own work, amazed other members, particularly those taking over some of her jobs.

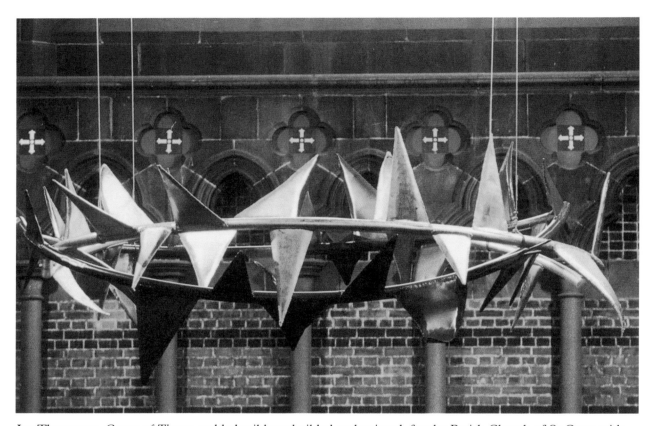

Ian Thompson, *Crown of Thorns*, welded mild steel gilded and painted, for the Parish Church of St Cross with St Paul, Clayton, Manchester

CHAPTER 12

2000 to 2003

The first exhibition of the twenty-first century in May 2000 attracted submissions from Russia, France and all parts of Britain, even the Orkney Isles. The show was opened by the popular *Coronation Street* actor, William Roache, who also presented the prizes; the major award that year went to David Frankel for his cast iron and bronze *Reliquary for Head of Judas*.

Work from recently elected members of all ages has enriched recent exhibitions and the Academy is thriving with one hundred and twenty-two members, and one hundred and fifteen subscribers.

Celebrations to mark the new millennium provided some Academicians with challenging projects. Don McKinlay was appointed to work on Luca Della

Norman Jaques, *River Medlock, Charles Street, Manchester*

Robbia's Madonna at the Anglican Cathedral in Liverpool. He has replaced, in his own style, the Christ Child, which was destroyed two hundred and fifty years ago. Glenys Latham carved a baptismal font for the 350-year-old Chowbent Unitarian Chapel, Atherton, where Alan Brough's sculpture, *Rebirth*, had been given sanctuary during the Second World War. The inspiration for the font came from observations of weathered tree skeletons and wave forms during her stay, funded by a MAFA bursary, on the Pacific coast of America. As part of The Millenium Year of the Artist project Julia Midgley made documentary drawings at Granada Television, and took on a long-term placement at Blackpool Pleasure Beach, with a studio in Goldmine Gully!

The newly refurbished Manchester Art Gallery was due to open. Members of the Academy were unsure of their place in the new regime. At an impassioned Extraordinary General Meeting

Alastair C. Adams, *Amy and Lucy*

in December 2001 the Director of the Gallery, Virginia Tandy, and Howard Smith, Head of Curatorial Services, met members and dealt with their questions. Although wishing to maintain a relationship with MAFA, the gallery's new commitments meant that this would not be a regular one. It later became clear that an alternative venue should be found for the Annual Open Exhibition which the members felt was an essential part of the Academy. However the cordial relationship with the gallery is ongoing; there was a selected exhibition of members' work in July and August 2003, and successful painting and drawing workshops have taken place with more planned.

The Annual Open Exhibition will be relaunched in March 2004 at Salford Art Gallery. Integral to the schedule of future exhibitions here will be educational opportunities. The popular lectures and workshops organised in recent years by Alastair Adams will be developed as well as links with schools and the adjacent university. But the main event remains the Open Exhibition acknowledged as the largest and most prestigious in the north. The ability of the Academy to adapt to changing circumstances while remaining true to its original aims has been its strength throughout a history spanning one hundred and forty-four years. A new, dynamic phase is about to begin.

Presidents of the Manchester Academy of Fine Arts

1858–62 James Astbury Hammersley   1862–5 John Lamont Brodie
1865–78 William Knight Keeling

1878–91
Robert Crozier

1891–2
Elias Bancroft

1892–1912
Clarence Whaite

1913–15
John Ely

1917–20
Tom Mostyn

1920–3
Francis Dodd

1923–34
Bertram Nicholls

1934–45
James Chettle

1945–8
Thomas Dugdale

1948–51
Charles
Oppenheimer

1951–60
John Gauld

1961–9
Harry Rutherford

1969–78
Roger Hampson

1978–84
Keith Godwin

1984–90
Norman Jaques

1990–3
Glenys Latham

1993–7
Peter Oakley

1997–2003
Ian Thompson

2003
John McPake

List of Members

with dates of their election since the foundation of the Academy

H = Honorary

1998	Adams, Alastair *RP*
1968 H	Adams, Norman *RA*
1925	Adin, C. Waldo
1871	Adshead, Joseph
1859	Agar, Charles
1926	Aitken, John E., *RSW, RCA, ARAW*
1932	Allan, Ronald, *FRSA*
1952	Allsop, George N.
1857	Anthony, George W.
1881	Armstrong, Thomas, *CB*
1940	Arnold, Patience
1882	Artingstall, William, *RCA*
1998	Aston, Paul
1900	Atcherley, Ethel
1921	Atherton, John Smith
1962	Bailey, Catherine
1964	Bailey, Terrance
1958	Bailey, William
1936	Balmford, Hurst
1988	Barnett, Lord Barnett
1872	Bancroft Elias, *RCA* (President 1892)
1899	Bancroft, Louisa M., *ARCA, FRSA*
1948	Bannon, Stanley
1973	Barber, Isobel, *FRSA*
1888	Barber, Reginald
1990	Bariow, Bohuslav
1879	Barker, W.D, *RCA*
1873	Barlow, T. Oldham, *RA*
1866	Barnes, J.H.
1998	Bartholomew, James
1942	Barton, Leonard, *ARCA*
1923	Baxter, David A.
1932	Baxter, Leslie R.
1926	Bayes, Gilbert, *HRI, FRBS*
1947	Bayes, Walter, *RWS*
1969	Bell, Vera
1943	Bennett, Harold, *RI, NRD*
1905	Birch, S. Lamorna, *RA*
1864	Blackwell, Isaac
1951	Bold, John, *RCA*
1961	Bonner, A.H. Lonsdale
1898	Booth, James W., *RCA*
1857	Bostock, John

1878	Bottomley, R.O.
1991	Bottomley, Vincent
1961	Boulton, Emeline (Mrs O'Brien)
1931	Boumphrey, Pauline
1931	Bowen, Owen, *ROI, PPRCA*
1938	Bowes, John, *RCA*
1864	Bowman, Henry
1880	Bradley, Basil, *RWS*
1941	Bradley, Frank, *RCA*
1951	Bradshaw, Brian, *Prix de Rome ARE, ARCA*
1884	Breakell, Mary L.
1952	Breton, Edith Le
1886	Brett, John, *ARA*
1938	Broadhead, Marion E.
1857	Brodie, J. Lamont (President 1862–5)
1868	Brookes, Warwick
1940	Brooks, Louie (Mrs Grimshaw)
1928	Brough, Alan
1883 H	Brown, Ford Madox
1998	Brown, Jo
1990	Brown, Keith
1952	Brown, Reg. V.
1985	Browne, Michael
1915	Bryce, Alexander J.C., *RBA*
1948	Buckley, Sydney
1959	Bunce, W.H. Stephen
1998	Burgess, Jane
1969	Buss, David
1941	Butterworth, Walter
2001	Byrne, Nicholas
1923	Cadness, Henry
1880	Caldecott, Randolph, *RI*
1857	Calvert, Henry
1910	Capper, Prof. Stewart H., *ARIBA*
1862	Cardwell, Holme
1883	Carrington, J. Yates
1965	Cartledge, Mary L.
1927	Cartledge, William
1934	Carver, Grace

1888	Cassidy, John, *RCA, RBS*
1984	Cebertowicz, Janina
1912	Chapman, Elizabeth M., *FRSA*
1903	Charles, James
1864	Charlesworth, John, *FRIBA*
1930	Chettle, James P., *RBA* (President 1934–45)
1958	Chirnside, John, *FRSA*
1960	Christopherson, Jose (Mrs Weisbrod)
1951 H	Churchill, The Rt. Hon. Sir Winston S., *KG, OM, CH, RA, MP*
1996	Clahane, Daniel
1937 H	Clark of Saltwood, The Lord, *CH, KCB, FBA*
1932	Clause, William
1922	Cockram, George, *RI, RCA*
1898	Cole, Chisholme, *RCA*
1878	Cole, J.H. *RCA*
1928	Colles, Elizabeth Orme
1932	Collin, Frank
1881	Collinson, Robert, *RCA*
1875	Cook, H. Moxon
1998	Cook, Nalini
1891	Cooper, Byron
1995	Cooper, Lucien
1932	Copley, John, *PPRBA, RE*
1940	Coupe, Fred
1936	Coventry, Gertrude (Mrs Robertson)
1958	Crabbe, Richard, *ARCA*
1977	Crabtree, Trevor, *RCA*
1993	Craddock, Adrienne
1981	Critchley, Harold W.
1984	Critchley, Paul
1995	Crook, Pam
1901	Crook, T. Mewburn, *RBS, ARCA*
1951	Crossley, Bob
1884	Crozier, Ann Jane
1870	Crozier, George, *RCA*
1857	Crozier, Robert (President 1878–91)

1970	Crummack, Jean C.
1923	Cundall, Charles E., *RA, RWS*
1951	Cusa, N.W.
1949	Daniels, Leonard W.
1997	Daniels, Lesley
1867	Darbyshire, Alfred, *MIBA*
1955	Davies, Austin
1894	Davies, Colley A.H., *MSA*
1873	Davies, James Hey, *RCA*
1945	Davies, John R., *RI*
1992	Dawes, Ian
1932	Deakin, Mabel G.
1954	Deane, Frederick A.
1981	Dewsbury, Sheila, *FRSA*
1937	Dimelow, Amy B.C.
1964	Dobbin, Stanley
1903	Dodd, Francis, *RA, RWS* (President 1920–3)
1947	Dodman, Frank
1956	Dolby, James T., *ARE, ARCA*
1998	Downhill, Kate
1994	Duffy, Terry
1910	Dugdale, Thomas C., *RA, RP* (President 1945–8)
1879	Dumaresq, Chev. Armand
1859	Duval, Charles A.
1956	Dyson, Douglas K., *ARCA*
1998	Easby, Steve
1979	Eastwood, Roger
1995	Edge, Peter
1962	Eley, William
1863	Elmore, Alfred, *RA*
1985	Elstein, Cecile
1899	Ely, John, *FRIBA* (President 1912–15)
1914	Emsley, Walter
1898	Enderby, Sam G.
1879	Estall, W. Charles
1999	Evans, Glynn
1999	Evans, Helen
1994	Exall, Michael
1932	Fairhurst, Enoch, *RMS*
1943	Ferguson, Hazel
1972	Fielding, Catherine
1974	Finn, Elizabeth
2000	Firmstone, David, *MBE*
1951	Fish, Gordon N.

1950	Fitton, Harvey
1948	Fitton, James, *RA*
1932	Flinn, Doris
1945	Forrester, Anna H.
1940	Foulkes, Mary H.
1999	Frankel, David
2001	Fuller, Gregory
1934	Gabain, Ethel, *ROI, RBA*
1940	Garside, John
1917	Garside, Oswald, *RI, RCA*
1936	Gauld, John R., *ARCA* (President 1951–60)
2002	Genner-Crawford, Anne
1936	Ghilchik, David L.
1940	Ghilchik, Josephine
1859	Gibson, J.V.
1906	Gilchrist, Philip T., *RBA*
1994	Gledhill, John
1975	Goddard, Michael
1973	Godwin, Keith, *RBA, ARCA* (President 1978–84)
1996	Golphin, Janet, *RWS, RBA*
1885	Goodfellow, Alfred
1945	Grant, Ian, *ARCA, FRSA*
1982	Green, Lorna, *FRBS*
1977	Greenhalgh, Kenneth
1930	Greenwood, John, *ARE*
1932	Greg, Barbara, *RE* (Mrs Janes)
1954	Gresty, Kenneth, *FRSA*
1957	Gribble, Kenneth, *FRSA*
1933	Grimmond, William
1978	Grimshaw, Trevor
1962	Gumuchian, Margaret, (Mrs Grant), *FRSA*
1864	Hadfield, Henry H.
1933	Hagedorn, Karl, *RI, RBA*
1873	Hague, Anderson, *RI, VPRCA*
1916	Hague, Dick, *RCA*
1873	Hague, J. Houghton
1922	Hall, Ethel
1995	Halliday, Irene, *RSW*
2001	Halpin, Gerry
1976	Hamlett, Keith
1857	Hammersley, J.A., *FRSA* (President 1859–62)
1958	Hampson, Roger H., *FRSA* (President1969–78)
2002	Hancock, David

2002	Hatjoulis, Michael C.
1999	Haworth, Derek
1859	Hayes, George, *RCA*
1947	Hemingway, Harold
1998	Henderson, Sue
1923	Henriques, Ethel Q.
1902	Henshall, J. Henry, *RWS*
1938	Henshaw, Lindley, *MC*
1968 H	Herman, Josef, *OBE, RA*
1961	Hewinson, J. Morgan, *ARCA*
1932	Hewitt, Forrest, *RBA*
1873	Heys, Ward
1922	Heywood, Brookes
1946	Hill, Thomas G.
1966	Hodgkinson, George
1921	Hoggatt, William, *RI, RBC*
1938	Holden, Dr Charles, *FRIBA*
1859	Holden, Isaac
1955	Holden, John H., *ARCA, RBSA*
1861	Holding, Henry J.
1923 H	Holmes, Sir Charles J.
1984	Holt, Charlie
1861	Hook, Richard
1888	Hopwood, H.S., *ARWS*
1906	Houghton, Elizabeth E.
1950	Howard, John D., *FRSA*
1958	Hughes, Kenneth L.
1952	Hughes, Malcolm, *ARCA*
1857	Hull, William
1988	Ibbotson, Pam
1936	Irwin, Greville, *RBA*
1881	Jackson, Frederick W.
1936	Janes, Norman, *RE, ARWS*
1950	Jaques, Norman C., *MSIA* (President 1984–90)
1981	Johnson, Colin T.
1999	Johnson, Derek C.
1907	Johnson, W. Noel
1874	Johnston, W. Herbert
1982	Jones, Alan George
1970	Jones-Hughes, Michelle
1970	Jones-Hughes, Selwyn
1998	Judd, Ian, *ARBS*
1857	Keeling, W. Knight (President 1865–78)
2001 H	Kent, Rev. Graham
1968	Key, Geoffrey, *G.B.*

1933	Kirk, Janet
1921	Knight, Joseph
1868	Knight, Joseph, *RI, RE, RCA*
1945	Knighton-Hammond, A.H., *RI, ROI, RWS*
1888	Knowles, G. Sheridan, *RI*
1923 H	Lamb, Henry, *MC, ARA*
1916	Lancaster, Percy, *RI, ARE, RCA*
1937	Langdon, Beatrice, *RCA*
1982	Latham, Glenys, *CIE* (President 1990-3)
1985	Lawson, Chris
1980	Lee, Graham J.
1922 H	Lee, Sydney, *RA, RE*
1934	Leech, Beatrice, M.S.
1937	Leeming, Matthew R.
1937	Leigh, Ethel Ashton
1882	Letherbrow, John Henry
1932	Levy, Emmanuel
1879	Lindsay, Sir Coutts, *Bart*
2001 H	Livesey, Joan
1983 H	Livesey, Philip, *FCA*
1870	Livett, L. Charles
1965	Lofthouse, Trevor B.
1891	Lomax, John A., *RBA*
1900	Longshaw, Frank W., *RCA*
1980	Lowe, Doreen
2001	Lowe, Kathleen
2002	Lowe, Katy
1975	Lowe, Vera
1935	Lowry, Laurence S., *RA, RBA*
1941	Luxmoore, John M.
1996	Lyons, Michael, *RBS*
1993	Ma, Yvonne
1975	McCombs, John, *RBA, ROI, FRSA*
1949	McGlynn, Terry
1984	McGuinness, Cornelius
1990	McKinlay, Donald
1999	McPake, John (President 2003)
1964	MacTaggart, Sir William, *PPRSA, LLD*
1992	Mackey, Stephen
1884	Magnus, Emma
1885	Magnus, Rose
1942	Maitland, Prof. Hugh B.

1952	Major, Theodore
1998	Mallett, Colin
1954	Malpass, J.C.L., *AMSA*
1994	Manby, Simon
1968	Mann, Robert
1986	Marsden, Grahame
1867	Marsh, Arthur, *ARWS*
1992	Martin, Deborah
1967	Martin, Patty
1977	Mason, Michael
1940	Massey, Delia V.
1962	Mather, Lady Eleanor
1898	Mavrogordato, Alex. J.
1869	Measham, Henry, *RCA*
1963	Medina Margarita
1936	Melland, Sylvia
2000	Melton, Stephen
1865	Mercier, Charles
1874	Meredith, William, *RCA*
1985	Midgley, Julia
1919	Millard, John (Officier d'Académie de France)
1930	Miller, W. Ongley, *ARCA*
1928	Milne, Malcolm
1942	Milner, Joseph
1857	Mitchell, Charles H.
1889	Monkhouse, M. Florence
1925	Mooney, E. Hartley
1995 H	Moorhouse, Cliff
1996	Morison, Rosemary
1890	Morris, C. Greville
1869	Morris, W. Bright
1941	Mort, Marjorie
1862	Morton, William
1895	Mostyn, Tom, *ROI, RA, RWA, RBA* (President 1916–20)
1881	Muckley, William J.
1961	Mumford, Sheila
2000	Murdoch, Keith
1932	Myers, Christina
1914	Nicholls, Bertram, *PPRBA* (President 1923–34)
1925	Nicholson, Albert
2002	Niemire, Patricia
1922	Noar, Eva, *RMS*
1988	Nolan, Brian
1926	Nowell, A.T., *RI, RPS*
1961	O'Brien, Ivor
1988	O'Reilly, Joseph

1987	Oakley, Peter (President 1993–7)
1911	Oppenheimer, Charles, *RSA, RSW* (President 1948–51)
1923 H	Orpen, Sir William, *KBE, RA*
1931	Owen, Joseph, *RSW, RWS*
1952	Owens, Ned
1927	Park, John A., *ROI, RBA*
1873	Partington, J.H.E.
1863	Paton, Sir Noel J., *RSA*
1989	Pearson, Christine
1936	Percy, Ida (Mrs Bond)
1857	Percy, William
1973	Picking, John
1926	Pilkington, Margaret, *OBE*
1959	Platt, Stella
1959	Pointon, Rhoda, *ARIBA*
1864	Potter, Charles, *RCA*
1935	Potts, Walter, *FRSA*
1872 H	Poynter, Sir E.J., *PRA*
1976	Radford, Gordon
1941	Rankin, Catherine
1989	Ratcliffe, Anthony
1876	Rathjens, William
1943	Rayner, Donald L., *RBA, RI*
1933	Reade, A. Vincent
1872	Redfern, Richard
1864	Redford, James, *MIBA*
1961 H	Redpath, Anne, *OBE, ARA, RSA*
1932	Reekie, W. Maxwell, *OBE*
1933	Rhodes, E. Millicent
1954	Rhodes, Marion E., *RE*
1945	Richardson, Edward H.
1940	Riding, Harold, *RCA*
1961	Riley, Harold F.
1996	Ritchie, Paul
1919	Roberts, Lancelot, *RCA*
1974	Roberts, Tony
1867	Robinson, George T., *FRIBA*
2001	Robinson, Kay
1879	Robinson, William
1998	Rogers, Alison
1958	Roocroft, Edward
1861	Rothwell, Selim
1977	Rowland, Dawn S., *FRBS*

1910	Royle, Herbert	1978	Taylor, Donald, Rome Scholar, *PDFA, DAD*	1932	Whaley, Harold A.
1922	Rushbury, Henry, *RA*			1932	Wheatley, Maurice, *ARCA*
1937	Russell, Jessie	1976	Taylor, James S., *FRSA, ARCA*	1886	Whitehead, Richard H.
1933	Rutherford, Harry (President 1961–9)			1988	Whittaker, Malcolm
		1984	Taylor-Wilson, Joanne	1999	Wild, Stephen
		1987	Thompson, Alan	1921	Wildman, William A., *RWS*
1859	Salomons, Edward, *FRIBA*	1990	Thompson, Ian (President 1997–2003)	1960	Wilkinson, Clifford, *ARCA*
1969	Sandiford, Adrian			1959	Wilkinson, Derek H.
1932	Schwabe, Randolph, *NEAC*	1884	Thomson, E. Gertrude	1970	Williams, Peter, *ATD*
		1999	Titherington, Tom	1972	Williams, Matti
1995	Scull, Paul	1958	Tocher, William E., *DFA*	1989	Woods, Brian
1932	Sellars, J. Henry	1932	Trench, Marianne L.	1937	Workman Harold, *RBA*
1990	Shaw, Andrew	1995	Tucker, Judith	1950 H	Worthington, Sir Hubert, *RA, OBE*
1963	Shaw, Peter	1929	Tunnicliffe, Charles F., *RA, RE, ARCA*		
1942	Shaw, T. Murray			1993	Wouda, Marjan
1872	Sheffield, George	1980	Turner, William, *FRSA, RCA*	1904	Wright, Gertrude E.
1859	Shields, Frederick J.			1973	Wright, Jack, *ARCA*
1990	Shutt, David	1950	Tuson, Robert	1896	Wroe Mary McNicholl
1862	Sidley, Samuel, *RBA*				
1938	Simm, William N., *AMC, MSA*	1919	Unwin, Frances Mabelle	1949	Yates, Hal, *RI, NS*
		1921	Unwin, Francis S.	1986	Yeomans, Michael
1994	Singh, Amrit				
1994	Singh, Rabindra	1938	van der Veen, C.W., *RCA*	1876	Zychlinski, Leo von
1997	Skinner, John	1934	Vasey, Gladys, *ARCA*		
1877	Slater, W.J., *RCA*	1979	Vivis, Geoffrey M., *RCA*		
1999	Smart, Anthony				
1969	Smith, Audrey	1870	Wake, Joseph		
1930	Smith, Reginald, *RWS, RSW*	1932	Walker, B. Eyre		
		1882	Walker, W. Eyre, *ARE, RWS*		
1973	Smith, Robert James				
1873	Somerset, Richard G., *RCA, ROI*	1994	Wallace, Lois		
		1875	Wallace, R. Bruce		
1960	Spafford, Iola, *RCA*	1917	Wallis, Hugh		
1985	Sprakes, John, *ROI*	1859	Ward, Charles		
2000	Stanaway, Peter	1898	Ward, Cyril, *RCA*		
1995	Stanley, David	1961	Ward, John		
1923	Steinthal, Bertha N.	1947	Warden, Arnold Forrester		
2000	Stephens, Terry	1946	Washington, William		
1873	Stephenson, James	1882	Wasse, Arthur		
1937	Stewart, Gilbert P.	1861	Waterhouse, Alfred, *FRIBA, RA*		
1941	Stokes, Amelia E.				
1947	Stokes, George W., *FRSA*	1868	Watson, J. Dawson, *RWS*		
1890	Stott Edward, *ARA*	1931	Weaver, Herbert P., *RBA, RCA, RWA*		
1887	Stott William, *RSW*				
1897	Sugars, Fanny	1922	Webster, W.E., *ROI, RI*		
1998	Sumner, Adrian	1989	Weir, Linda		
1877	Swynnerton, Joseph	1958	Weisbrod, Richard		
1884	Swynnerton, Annie L., *ARA*	2001	West, Ulrich		
		1859	Whaite, H. Clarence, *PRCA, RWS* (President 1892–1912)		
1998	Sykes, Barbara				
1981	Sykes, George				

Index

Acomb Street 40, 41, 56
Adams, Alastair 85
Adams, Norman 63, 68, 79
Agnew Art Dealers 23, 42, 56
Allan, Ronald 54
Anthony, George W. 13
Artingstall, William 20
Associated Artists of Manchester 9, 10, 11
Atheneum 53, 66, 69, 71, 79

Bailey, William 60
Barber, Reginald 27
Barlow, Bohuslav 73
Bancroft, Elias 25, 27, 31, 32, 41
Bancroft, Louisa M. 25, 27, 31, 41
Barry, Sir Charles 9, 66
Bates, Merete 68
Birch, S. Lamorna 59
Bold, John 54, 56, 68
Bone, Muirhead 40, 56
Bostock, John 12
Bowen, Owen 23, 53
Bowness, Alan 71
Bradshaw, Brian 53, 56, 59
Brazenose Street 20
Breton, Edith Le 53
Brodie, John Lamont 12, 13
Brough, Alan 44, 46, 83
Brown, Ford Madox 16, 25, 59
Browne, Michael 79, 80
Burns, Richard 81, 82
Bury Art Gallery 56, 81, 82

Calvert, Henry 13
Cassidy, John 25, 27, 30, 60
Castlefield 30, 70
Cebertowicz, Janina 80, 81
Chetham's School 15, 27
Chettle, James 44, 46, 59
Chowbent Unitarian Chapel 46, 83
Christopherson, Jose 54, 61
Churchill, Sir Winston 57, 62
Clahane, Danny 79
Clark, Sir Kenneth, Lord Clark of Saltwood 62

Clause, William 48
Clifford, Jane 68, 69
Clifford, Timothy 69
Coldstream, William 62
Conran, L. George 63
Cooper, Byron 42
Copley, John 42, 48
Cornerhouse 72
Crane Gallery 56
Critchley, Paul 71, 73
Cross Street Unitarian Chapel 46
Crozier, Ann 17
Crozier, Robert 10, 12, 20
Cundall, Charles 36, 44, 46, 48

Dacre, S. Isabel 17, 36, 38, 40, 41, 42
Dagnall, Thompson 79
Daily Mail 36
Daily Telegraph 68, 69
Darbyshire, Alfred 16
Deane, Frederick 59, 63
Delaney, Arthur 68
Dobbin, Stanley 75
Dodd, Francis 32, 36, 38, 39, 40, 41, 48, 59
Drumcroon Arts Centre 75, 76
Dugdale, Thomas 32, 48

Edge, Peter 80
Ely, John 30, 32

Festival of Britain 54, 56
Fitton, James 57, 59
Frankel, David 83

Gabain, Ethel 42, 46, 48
Gallery of Modern Art 69, 71, 79
Gauld, John 57, 62
Gibb's bookshop 53, 60
Godwin, Keith 69
Golphin, Janet 79
Granada Foundation 66
Grant, Ian 53, 54, 56, 63, 72
Gray, Richard 82
Green, Geoffrey 60, 61

Green, Jan 61
Grimmond William 48
Guardian, The 60, 68, 75
Gumuchian, Margaret 56, 63, 72

Hagedorn, Karl 48, 53
Hague, Anderson 14, 20, 22, 34
Hague, Houghton 42
Halliday, Irene 63, 79
Hamlett, Keith 70, 73
Hammersley, James Astbury 10, 11, 12, 13, 56
Hampson, Roger 53, 59, 61, 63, 66, 68
Hasling, Annie 17,
Haward Lawrence 32, 44, 46, 48, 49, 66
Hayes, George 14, 20
Herman, Josef 63
Hewinson, Morgan 63
Hewitt, Forest 44
Holden, John 56, 57
Holmes, Sir Charles 36
Hull, William 13, 14

Ingham, Margo 41, 53, 54, 63, 66
Irving, Sir Henry 16

Jackson, Frederick 14, 30, 42
Jaques, Norman 53, 54, 57, 63, 68, 71, 72, 75
Jellicoe, Colin 66, 76
Julien, Monsieur 25, 54

Kalman, Andreas 69
Keeling, William Knight 13, 16
Key, Geoffrey 66, 67
Kirk, Janet 56
Knight, Joseph [elected 1868] 14
Knight, Joseph [elected 1921] 39
Knowles, Sheridan 32
Kroch, Carol 68

Lamb, Henry 36, 40, 48, 49
Latham, Glenys 70, 73, 83
Lee, Sydney 36

Levy, Emmanuel 42, 53, 59
Livesey, Philip 72
Lowe, Vera 72, 73, 82
Lowndes, Alan 53, 69
Lowry, L.S. 23, 34, 36, 42, 44, 48, 53, 54, 56, 59, 66, 67, 69, 72
Lyons, Michael 70, 79

McComb, Leonard 63
McCombs, John 61, 68, 73, 81
McGlynn, Terry 53, 54, 56, 58, 61, 63
McKinlay, Donald 73, 83
Ma, Yvonne 75
Magnus, Emma 27, 42
Magnus, Rose 14
Major, Theodore 53, 54, 56
Manby, Simon 79
Manchester City Art Gallery 9, 10, 20, 25, 27, 29, 30, 31, 32, 34, 36, 38, 40, 42, 44, 46, 48, 53, 56, 59, 63, 66, 68, 69, 72, 79, 80, 81, 82, 83
Manchester City News 32
Manchester Evening News 20, 42, 44, 50, 69, 73, 80
Manchester Examiner 14
Manchester Guardian 11, 13, 14, 17, 30, 32, 34, 39, 41, 44, 46, 48, 56, 58, 59, 60
Manchester Jewish Museum 15
Manchester Polytechnic 57, 68, 71
Manchester Regional College of Art 41, 54, 56, 57, 60, 65, 66, 72
Manchester School, The 14, 20
Manchester School of Art 10, 13, 20, 27, 36, 38, 56
Manchester School of Design 9, 10, 56
Manchester Town Hall 15, 16, 29, 42, 59
Manchester University 15, 32, 57, 71, 72, 80
Massey, Delia 53, 56
Measham, Henry 20
Medina, Margarita 58, 61
Meredith, Charles 14, 20
Midday Studios 41, 53, 54, 60, 66, 72

Midgley, Julia 75, 80, 83
Mitchell, Charles 13
Monkhouse, Florence 40
Monnington, Sir Tom 68
Moorhouse, Cliff 81
Morris, William 20
Mostyn, Tom 32, 42
Muckley, William 38

Nicholls, Bertram 36, 41, 42
Noar, Eva 40
Nolan, Brian 61, 63
North Wales 14, 22, 23
Northern Arts Foundation 66
Northern School, The 53, 54, 56, 68

Oakley, Peter 74, 75
Observer, The 44
O'Reilly, Joseph 73
Orpen, Sir William 32, 36
Owens, Ned 53, 54, 59

Parkes, Geoffrey 62
Peel Park, Salford 11
Percy, William 10, 12, 14, 59
Peterloo 9, 16
Piccadilly Gardens 25, 66
Pilkington, Margaret 36, 44, 49
Portico Library and Gallery 36, 76, 78
Potter, Charles 20, 22
Prince Albert 11, 12, 13

Queen Victoria 11, 13, 23
Queen's Park Art Gallery 25, 69

Rayner, Donald 62, 69
Redpath, Anne 62
Reekie, W. Maxwell 44, 53
Renold Building, UMIST 68
Riley, Harold 61, 63, 67
Ritchie, Paul 75
Robert-Blunn, John 69, 73
Robinson, Emily 17
Robinson, Julia 17
Roocroft, Ted 60, 63, 65, 70, 73, 80
Rowland, Dawn 70, 79

Royal Cambrian Academy 23, 27, 34, 42
Royal Manchester Institution [RMI] 9, 10, 11, 13, 14, 15, 16, 19, 20, 27, 53, 56, 66
Ruskin, John 15
Rutherford, Harry 42, 53, 62, 63, 65, 68
Rylands Library 25

Salford Art Gallery 56, 59, 66, 68, 69, 70, 76, 85
Salford Technical School 27
Salford University 68, 85
Salisbury Heywood, Mrs. E 66
Salomons, Edward 15, 63
Schwabe, Randolph 48, 53, 54
Scott, C.P 39
Sewter, Alan 58, 59
Shaw, Peter 63
Sheppard Robson 68
Shields, Frederick 10, 15
Shuttleworth, Peter 68
Sickert, Walter 53, 65
Singh, Amrit 79
Singh, Rabindra 79
Smith, Howard 85
Somerset, Richard Gay 14, 20
Southworth, Mary 17
Spafford, Iola 23, 63, 68
Spalding, Julian 72
Sprakes, John 73
Spratley and Cullearn 68
Stanaway, Peter 79
Stanley, David 78, 79
Stott, Edward 25
Stott, William 25, 42
Subscribers of MAFA 27, 63, 83
Sugars, Fanny 42
Swynnerton, Annie L 17, 36, 39, 42
Swynnerton Joseph W 36, 60
Sykes, George 73

Tandy, Virginia 85
Thompson, Ian 80
Thomson, E. Gertrude 17
Tib Lane Gallery 61, 76

Titherington, Tom   73-4
Tunnicliffe, Charles   36, 59
Turner, William   53, 61
Tuson, Robert   53

Valette, Adolphe   36, 65
Vasey, Gladys   59

Wasse, Arthur   25
Waterhouse, Alfred   15, 16
Weir, Linda   79
Weisbrod, Richard   53, 54
Whaite, Clarence   10, 12, 13, 14,
    22, 23, 25, 27, 30, 60
Whitworth Art Gallery   30, 36, 49,
    56
Whitworth Park   25, 40
Wilkinson, Derek   59, 61, 63, 75,
    81
Williams, Terrick   36
Williamson, Harold   62
Wood, Eleanor   17, 31
Wood, Warrington   25
Wood, Wilfred   63
Woods, Brian   72
Workman, Harold   48, 53, 56
Worthington, Sir Hubert   57
Wright, Gertrude E   42

Yates, Hal   53, 60, 62, 67, 68, 69